DISCOVER NEW YORK
WITH HELEN WORDEN

Sketches by HELEN WORDEN

AMERICAN
WOMEN'S
VOLUNTARY
SERVICES

☆ *CONTENTS* ☆

Foreword:
THE AMERICAN WOMEN'S VOLUNTARY SERVICES

Published in Great Britain in 2013 by Old House books & maps
Midland House, West Way, Botley, Oxford OX2 0PH, United Kingdom.
4301 21st Street, Suite 220B, Long Island City, NY 11101, USA.
Website: www.oldhousebooks.co.uk

A CIP catalogue record for this book is available from the British Library.

ISBN-13: 978 1 90840 265 3

Originally published in 1943 by the American Women's Voluntary Services.
Printed in China through Worldprint Ltd.

This is a facsimile reproduction of a publication first published in 1943 and
contains the common spelling and terms used in everyday language of that
period. The publisher has maintained the integrity of the original edition,
as is, to ensure that it is an accurate historical document of the time.

13 14 15 16 17   10 9 8 7 6 5 4 3 2 1

Foreword

☆

IN DEDICATING THIS BOOK *to the men and women of the Armed Forces, I should like to pay a tribute to Helen Worden whose untiring efforts have made it possible.*

This is the fourth New York guide book written by Miss Worden, who knows the city as few do. Her seventeen years of work on two of the city's largest newspapers, The World and the World-Telegram, have given her this unique knowledge. "The Real New York" was her first book; the second, "Round Manhattan's Rim," and the third, "Here Is New York" was the official guide book at the World's Fair.

This fourth, "Discover New York," Miss Worden is generously giving to the American Women's Voluntary Services so that all profits from it will go towards the support of the important work we are doing.

As our name implies, the spirit of the A.W.V.S. is service to the local community and to the country at large. In New York City, which many of you may be visiting for the first time, we want to help make your stay so pleasant that you will remember us for a long while to come. We of the A.W.V.S. wish all men and women in service to feel that we not only hope to be of assistance to them in any way we can, but that we are personally interested in everyone who may call upon us. We should like to meet you, not as members of an organization, but as friends.

This Guide Book has been prepared to aid you in finding our city's interest spots, as well as those special places where we can offer you service and recreation.

Welcome to our city! And a happy stay to you all!

ALICE T. McLEAN

American Women's Voluntary Services, Inc.

Board of Directors

OFFICERS

President, Mrs. Alice T. McLean
First Vice-President, Mrs. Ogden L. Mills
Vice-President, Mrs. Bernard F. Gimbel
Vice-President, Mrs. Stanhope Nixon
Vice-President, Miss Ruth V. Twombly
Treasurer, Mrs. Leroy A. Lincoln

BOARD OF DIRECTORS

Miss Mary Vail Andress
Dr. Adelaide Baylis
Miss Katherine L. Beach
Miss Dorothy Bellanca
Dr. Mary McLeod Bethune
Mrs. William C. Breed
Mrs. George Lewis Callery
Mrs. William F. Carey
Mrs. Robert L. Clarkson
Mrs. Bernard F. Gimbel
Mrs. William H. Hays
Mrs. Mortimer Hess
Mrs. T. Arnold Hill
Mrs. Josephine Hong
Mrs. Cornelius F. Kelley
Mrs. Daniel Kempner
Mrs. Isabella Greenway King
Mrs. John W. Lawrence
Mrs. Edgar Leonard
Miss Ruth Lewinson

Mrs. Leroy A. Lincoln
Mrs. Watson McLallen
Mrs. Alice T. McLean
Mrs. Audrey McMahon
Mrs. Ogden L. Mills
Mrs. Margery Newton
Mrs. Stanhope Nixon
Mrs. Louis W. Noel
Mrs. J. J. O'Brien
Mrs. Charles Payson
Miss Anita Phipps
Mrs. William A. Porteous
Mrs. Charles F. Robbins
Mrs. Mary Steele Ross
Miss Rose Schneiderman
Mrs. Harold Talbott
Miss Ruth V. Twombly
Mrs. Robert Winthrop
Mrs. William Woodward
Mrs. William Woolston

PRESENTING THE
A·W·V·S

YOU ARE going to meet the friendly ladies of the American Women's Voluntary Services many times during your New York sightseeing jaunts, for they get around. I find them in the most unexpected places doing helpful and interesting work. They are good neighbors. Their share in New York's community life is one of the reasons I am happy and proud to be able to join them in their aims with this work.

The A.W.V.S., as it is usually referred to, was founded in January, 1940 by a gentle-spoken and entirely un-aggressive person, Mrs. Alice Throckmorton McLean. She felt that there must be thousands of women like her who wanted to be ready to serve the communities in which they lived if and when war came.

There were. Before the end of 1940, over 100,000 women had signed up with the A.W.V.S. The first official meeting was held in a little basement antique shop at Cooperstown, N. Y., near Mrs. McLean's big farm. She and three other courageous women came to discuss their future work. Their pattern was the British Women's Voluntary Services.

Today the A.W.V.S. is a national organization with over 460 units, 90 different activities and more than

325,000 members. There are no dues. It is supported by contributions and by its activities, of which this guide is one. Mrs. William C. Breed, head of the A.W.V.S. benefits and activities, helped make the book possible.

The A.W.V.S. now members 124 units in Greater New York, with others in the process of formation. National Headquarters where Mrs. McLean has her busy office, are at 345 Madison Avenue. Other units will be mentioned as we reach their particular neighborhoods in this book.

Mark them well. They may come in handy. It's pleasant to know that you already have friends in strange neighborhoods of the biggest city in the world.

A.W.V.S.
INFORMATION

CHAPTER I

Our Transportation System

THERE HAVE been radical changes in New York's transportation system in recent years. Street car tracks were torn up and elevated railroads torn down. Motor buses replaced both.

The only trolley cars still functioning in the main part of Manhattan are the Broadway and Third Avenue routes. For five cents you can ride from the Bowery to Fort George or from 42nd Street and First Avenue to 125th Street and Broadway. It's as good a way as any to get an idea of the physical aspects of the city.

Another five cent tour can be made on the Third Avenue Elevated road, the only one left standing in New York. The most interesting run is from South Ferry to 241st Street, through the lower East Side, past midtown New York, across the Harlem River and on up to the Bronx.

Buses belong in the same leisurely category. You will find them running north and south on all but a few of the avenues, the principal exceptions being Park and West End Avenues. During the war many stop running at midnight. Fare on the Fifth Avenue and 57th Street crosstown buses is 10¢. On all the rest it is 5¢.

The subway is the most dependable and least inspiring form of New York transit. There are three main divisions, the IRT (Interborough Rapid Transit), which runs on the east and west sides, the BMT (Brooklyn Manhattan Transit) which connects most of Brooklyn with New York, and the Independent which is the newest and the most pleasant to ride upon.

I can give you general directions about the subways but actually, the only way to learn which line to take where, is to ask questions of the subway change clerks, study the car maps and ride on the trains.

The Lexington Avenue Subway runs on the East Side, the Broadway line on the West Side, the Sixth Avenue and Eighth Avenue to the Bronx and Washington Heights.

The name of the station is lettered on the pillars and worked in mosaics on the walls. The most interesting of all the subway stations is the least used—the Mayor's station at City Hall. The placque opposite the entrance gives the history of the subway.

Our bridges, highways and tunnels will be mentioned in detail as we come to them. The principal ones to remember are the George Washington, the Whitestone, Triborough and Brooklyn Bridges, the East and West Side Highways, and the Holland, Lincoln, and Queens Midtown Tunnels.

New York's plane traffic is handled through La Guardia Field, the N. Y. Municipal Airport, located on the meadows of Flushing, just outside the city limits. It is America's No. 1 airport, serving the big domestic airlines, including Eastern Air Lines, American Airlines, Transcontinental & Western Air and United, as well as

Arriving at La Guardia Field

the Trans-Atlantic service of Pan American and American Export Airlines. Main ticket offices for the airlines are in the Airlines Terminal Building at 42nd Street and Park Avenue, from which point the various airline buses go directly to the airport, leaving 40 minutes before plane departure.

A visit to the airport is entertaining even if you're not taking a plane. The Kitty Hawk room is very popular for cocktails. The promenade restaurant, (from your table on the terrace you can see the planes arriving and departing) is a unique place to eat.

As for railroad depots, there are two on Manhattan Island—the Grand Central at 42nd Street between Lexington and Vanderbilt Avenues and the Pennsylvania Station at Seventh Avenue and 33rd Street. The Lackawanna, Erie, Baltimore and Ohio, West Shore and Jersey Central Railroad Stations are on the New Jersey side of the Hudson River. They may be reached by ferry, bus or the Hudson Tubes.

Ferries also connect New York with Staten Island, Bedloe's Island and certain parts of Brooklyn.

One of the best views of the New York skyline is from the Staten Island Ferry. The sail, which costs a nickel, lasts twenty minutes. You'll find the Staten Island ferry at the foot of Manhattan Island at the southeast end of Battery Park.

In summer the Sightseeing Boat leaves from Pier One, Battery Park every day at 10:30 a.m. and 2:30 p.m. The sail around Manhattan Island takes two hours and costs $1.75. It's about the quickest way I know to get an idea of the widely varied sections of the city.

CHAPTER II

Our Streets and How to Find Them

THE STREETS of New York between Washington Square and Harlem are easy enough to locate. It is said that the Commissioners who laid them out got their idea from a sieve. They were walking over the unchartered portion of Manhattan Island discussing the matter when the eyes of one whose name nobody remembers, fell on the shadow cast by the sunlight shining through a gravel sieve.

"There's an idea!" he exclaimed. "Why not lay our streets out like that? Number those running east and west and make avenues out of those going north and south."

The first numbered streets were laid out in 1811 with Fifth Avenue for the dividing line. The plan has never changed. The only streets which don't extend west of it are Seventh and Sixth. Fifth, Second and First Streets are lost in the maze of Greenwich Village cow-paths.

There is no set rule for our street numbers, but the even numbers are usually on the south side and the odd on the north. For example, if you want to go to 154 West 57th Street, which happens to be Carnegie Hall, you can easily tell from the address that this is west of Fifth Avenue on the south side of 57th Street. Or, if you wish to find 205 East 42nd Street, the home of Yank, the army newspaper, you would look for it on the north side of 42nd Street east of Fifth Avenue.

The principal avenues are Fifth, which begins at Washington Square, Park which picks up where Fourth Avenue leaves off at 34th Street and Madison, whose fountain-head is 23rd Street.

Broadway is the only main thorofare running continuously from one end of Manhattan Island's thirty-four miles to the other.

Since the shadow of the sieve fell on that portion of the town which includes the most famous part of Broadway, we won't worry about the other sections of the city until we come to them.

You will need special directions for financial New York, the Lower East Side and Greenwich Village. Cows and not a sieve, were the path-finders here. Sometimes the irregular boundary lines of a farm like Peter Stuyvesant's further complicated the pattern.

CHAPTER III

Our Neighborhoods

OF COURSE New York is one big city, but those of us who know it well think of it as a series of villages.

In Colonial times that portion of Manhattan Island called New York barely reached beyond Trinity Church. Greenwich Village, Chelsea, Murray Hill, Yorkville, Harlem, Bloomingdale and Washington Heights were separate little towns. Even today when all these villages have become Greater New York the character of each is still pretty clearly defined.

The oldest section, financial New York, is the early Dutch settlement. The skyscrapers of Wall Street rim winding thorofares which trace the cow-paths and lanes of Peter Stuyvesant's day.

The Bowery, in those old Dutch times, was a charming suburban section. Later it became a charming street of iniquity. Now that it's tamed down it is still picturesque and legendary.

Greenwich Village, like financial New York, is a maze of winding streets which even New Yorkers can't find. It is also a neighborhood of cellar restaurants in which art is argued by the light of tallow candles. The artists who once made the Village famous now live in all parts of the city. But you'll see still enough picturesque characters to color an evening's visit. There are certain land-marks, Charles' restaurant is one, which always justify a trip to Greenwich Village.

Chelsea makes you think of Dickens' and Thackeray's London.

Murray Hill has an Edith Wharton atmosphere. You see plum colored, horse-drawn broughams parked in front of its brown stone stoops. You will also see the J. P. Morgan library, the Soldiers' and Sailors' Club and The American Red Cross headquarters.

Yorkville is a hodge-podge of Hungarian, Viennese, Czech, German and Irish with a good share of Fifth and Park Avenues tossed in. You'll find Bavarian beer halls and konditorei shops on East 86th Street and fine Viennese cafes on East 79th Street.

Harlem is in a class by itself. Forty years ago this section was almost a suburb of the city proper. It is now a densely populated city within a city—the chief negro district of New York. It also contains Puerto Ricans and Central Americans.

Bloomingdale lay just below what is now Columbia University. The University stands on what was once Harlem Heights.

North of Columbia, on the upper West side of Man-hattan Island, is Washington Heights, the great refugee center of the city. It is also famous for having been an early Indian camping ground.

There are many other fascinating sections which I will mention later but because most of the people who come to New York want to see Broadway first I am making it the starting point of our book. The very name is synony-mous with entertainment.

View of Broadway looking north from Times Square

· BROADWAY ·

THE NEIGHBORHOOD in which you are to begin your acquaintance with New York, Broadway, is one of the most famous in the world.

The stories and songs which have been written about it would fill a library.

While the street itself extends from the Battery to Spuyten Duyvil, the section referred to as "Broadway" runs only from 42nd to 50th Streets in the blocks between 6th and 8th Avenues. This is the heart of the theatrical district. All the big theaters, the dance halls, most of the night clubs and cafes are here.

Spasmodically, Broadway has been effected by the war. First, the lights went off then on. At the start, the crowds thinned out. But now, Broadway is having the greatest boom in its history.

Stand on the corner of 42nd Street and Broadway and watch the people. You'll see them by the thousands, all types and all kinds.

Times Square is still the heart of New York to the three million visitors who pour into the city every month.

The obvious places of entertainment like the Crossroads Cafe are easy enough to locate. Their addresses and prices will be mentioned in this chapter. You will also find listed the lesser-known little side-shows, restaurants and night clubs which to me, are the real Broadway.

*   *   *

THE SIDE-SHOWS OF 42nd STREET. Every other door in the block between 8th and 7th Avenues on 42nd Street, is a side-show. Good old-fashioned country circus barkers line the sidewalks shouting, "This way, Ladi-ees and Gentle-mennnn! The most wonderful show in town! See five dollars' worth for five cents!!"

The Side-Show of Shows is Hubert's Museum at 228 West 42nd Street. The admission is 15c.

Half a block east is that war-time hub, the Crossroads Cafe which serves fifty thousand a day.

TOFFENETTI'S is at 43rd and Broadway. This huge modernistic restaurant is jammed with diners by five o'clock in the afternoon. Prices are moderate—roast chicken, dessert and coffee, $1.25. Or you may have broiled lamb chops on the dinner for $1.45. An à la carte order of spaghetti with meat sauce is 50c.

MADISON SQUARE GARDEN, a present-day landmark, is at 8th Avenue and 50th Street. Keep an eye on it for sporting events, like prize fights and hockey games. The circus is also held here.

Across the street is Rogers' Corner, a convenient spot to eat before going to any Garden features. Dinners start at $1.50.

Jack Dempsey opened this restaurant, then went out of the business for a time. Now he is back at 1619 Broadway. Drop in before six if you want to see Jack. An average dinner at his new place costs about four dollars for two.

You will like the mussel soup, the home-made spaghetti inundated by clam and tomato sauce plentifully sprinkled with Parmesan cheese, the steamed devil-fish (it tastes like frogs' legs or the white meat of chicken) and the finely cooked broccoli simmered in drawn butter at Leone's, 239 W. 48th St. Dinners are from $2.50 up.

GREEK SETTLEMENT. From 42nd Street to 39th Streets between Eighth and Ninth Avenues, lies the largest Greek settlement in the city.

It offers you Greek maps, glittering ikons, Turkish Delight, strange little individual brass coffee-pots and spiced olives.

Jumbled in with the wholesale cloak and suit dealers, furriers, automobile license bureaus and taverns, fifty thousand Greeks eke out an existence.

SARDI'S. From the Greeks we turn to Sardi's, a restaurant made famous by the theatrical crowd at 234 West 44th Street. Here you will see actors, producers, playwrights, authors, angels and press-agents. The best time to go is around noon or just after the theater. Gard, the Russian cartoonist, sketched the celebrities that decorate the walls.

THE HOTEL ASTOR at 44th Street and Broadway is famous for its roof garden, a fine place to go hot summer nights. Dinner with dancing costs around $8.00 a couple.

46th STREET—DINTY MOORE'S. Everybody on Broadway knows Dinty Moore. His glittering brass and glass front food emporium at 216 West 46th Street is famous for beefsteak and onion sandwiches.

It is a central place for dinner and also a fine after-theater spot, a favorite with politicians, race-track men and actors. The food is very expensive. Hamburgers cost $2.00. Of course this includes a chance to see the celebrities.

THE RAJAH INDIA RESTAURANT. Mr. Wadia runs this East Indian restaurant at 235 West 48th Street.

The specialty of the house is curry and rice, Bombay duck, rose-petal coffee and tamarind. The duck isn't duck at all. Tamarind is a tropical drink. Mr. Wadia's dinners start at 75c.

DAVE'S BLUE ROOM. The sporting crowd hangs out at 60 West 52nd Street. If you try this place for a three-decker sandwich, you may find your favorite booky sitting across the table. Broadway columnists also frequent this restaurant.

LINDY'S. Don't mention Arnold Rothstein's name at 1626 Broadway. This is the restaurant where the gambler answered the famous phone call (booth still standing), that led him to make a date with Death.

Spitale and Bitz, the go-betweens in the Lindbergh kidnaping case, were also faithful patrons.

The food is good. I like the chopped liver and onion sandwiches on rye bread. The branch restaurant of this Lindy's at 51st Street and Broadway, draws the big race track crowd today. Average prices.

With the exception of Dinty Moore's, I have purposely avoided the more highly priced restaurants.

THE ALGONQUIN at 59 West 44th Street is famous as being the hotel which Frank Case runs. Mr. Case writes best sellers as well as manages a fine hotel. The midnight Welsh rabbits in which the hotel specializes are very good. So are all the meals.

The Algonquin is also noted for its celebrity clientele. The quality of Mr. Case's hospitality has been attracting stars in the literary and theatrical world. John Erskine, Joseph Hergesheimer, Fannie Hurst, Charles McArthur, Rita Weiman, Anna May Wong, Hedda Hopper—you'll see them all, sooner or later, at the Algonquin.

ST. MARY'S CHURCH. Another landmark in the Forties is St. Mary's Church at 139 West 46th Street. It is the highest Episcopal Church in New York as far as ritual goes, the only difference between it and the Catholic Church being that mass at St. Mary's is said in English instead of Latin. There is also a confessional in the church.

There is much of New York to see after midnight, but we won't try to do it all at once. The city from Brooklyn Bridge, the sky-line of 59th Street from the windows of a hansom jogging through Central Park, Little Italy on a Fiesta Night—but all that is a different story.

I want you to become thoroughly acquainted with the Forties before we put foot in another part of town.

TIN PAN ALLEY. Night or day you may hear the ivories being tickled if you stroll through 45th and 46th Streets west of Broadway. This is Tin-Pan Alley. A hundred or more popular song publishing houses hang out their shingles in this locality. Some, like Irving Berlin, have moved. His firm is now at 799 Seventh Avenue.

ARABIAN PERFUMES. Broadway has its exotic little shops. The Spaniard who runs the small shop at 145 West 44th Street is Mr. Francisco Compy, an importer of rare Arabian perfumes made from the flowers of the Sahara.

Mr. Compy also stocks silver jewelry made by desert tribes. It is enameled in bright colors. The bracelets run from $10.00 to $20.00 each. Another interesting article which he carries is the Arabian burnoose.

UNCLE SAM'S. If your umbrella won't open, your parasol needs scrubbing, or your malacca cane requires a new ferrule, call on Uncle Sam, at 110 West 45th Street. He does all manner of repairing in these lines, reasonably and well. This is a fascinating store—the oldest in the neighborhood. It carries sword canes.

THE HARMONY BOOK-SHOP is the place to go if you wish to have your fortune told. It is a tiny store wedged in between two larger shops at 112 West 49th Street. Here, amid all sorts of occult and ism literature, you will find a bulletin-board. On it are tacked the cards bearing names and addresses of leading astrologers and psychics in New York. The Harmony Shop also carries a complete stock of theosophical, astrological and occult books.

ANTIQUES. See Mrs. Trigger if you like odds and ends in jewelry, silverware, clothes, antiques or pictures. She buys from and sells to the theatrical crowd.

Over a counter at 47 West 44th Street she conducts a business established since 1897 and familiar to every second-hand-shop browser in New York.

THE HOUSE OF CHAN at 800 Seventh Avenue, caters to devotees of Chinese food. Sou Chan, the proprietor, raises the vegetables for his authentic Cantonese dishes on his thirty-eight acre Long Island farm. Ambassador Wellington Koo, ex-Ambassador Hu Shih, Lin Yutang, Fred Allen and Jimmy Braddock like to eat here when they're in town. Dinners start at $1.50.

· CANTEENS ·

AT THIS WRITING there are hundreds of canteens for the armed forces in the Broadway district. Canteen is a broad term that may mean a place to write a letter, get a meal, or dance.

A.W.V.S. 2-4-1 LUNCHEON CANTEEN. Open daily except Sundays, in the Green Room of the Hotel Edison, 228 West 47th Street, from 12 noon to 3 p.m. A true crossroads for service men and women of all the United Nations, this canteen is unique in that it offers those in our armed forces a place where they can play host to an invited guest. Members of the Merchant Marine are also welcome. Two moderate priced lunches are provided at the cost of one, hence the catchy name.

STAGE DOOR CANTEEN. One million, seven hundred and seventy thousand soldiers and sailors have already found their way to the theater's canteen at 224 West 44th Street. It is open from five to midnight seven days a week. There is entertainment, dancing and refreshments (sandwiches, coffee, pie, cigarettes, etc.) and no charge for anything. No pass is needed. Men in uniform are asked to show their identification card to keep out phonies.

MERCHANT SEAMEN'S CLUB at 107 West 43rd Street is also sponsored by the American Theatre Wing and is similar to the Stage Door Canteen.

TIMES SQUARE SERVICE MEN'S CENTER at 1572 Broadway (45th Street at the intersection of Broadway and 7th Avenue) offers checking, rest rooms, showers, voice recordings and Pepsi Cola without charge. Hamburgers are 5c.

THE FRENCH SEAMEN'S FOYER at 63 West 44th Street is open from 2 p.m. to 11 p.m. on week days and from 11 a.m. to 11 p.m. on Sunday. Canteen serves red wine, coffee and sandwiches.

THE AIR FORCE CLUB at 55 West 44th Street is open every day from 9 a.m. to 11 p.m. to all men in the air forces of the United Nations. Their wives are also welcome. There are club room facilities including a reading and writing room. You may use the showers without charge. Tea is served.

THE BRITISH MERCHANT NAVY OFFICERS CLUB at 55 West 44th Street, is for officers and petty officers of the merchant marine. Although primarily for the British, others are welcome. The hours are 11 a.m. to 11 p.m. every day except Friday when the club remains open until 1 a.m.

THE UNION JACK CLUB on the second floor of 587 Fifth Avenue (at 48th Street) is open from 9:30 a.m. to 11 p.m. In addition to sailors and petty officers of the British Royal Navy, British army men are welcome. Here you can obtain free tickets for movies, entertainments and dances.

ANZAC CLUB at 106 West 56th Street, is open from 9 a.m. to 10:30 p.m. to all officers and servicemen from Australia and New Zealand. Miss Nola Luxford, an enterprising New Zealander, originated the club two years ago in her own home on East 38th St. When it outgrew those quarters last year, the group moved to its present location in the Phi Gamma Delta Fraternity House.

Tea is served free at 4:30 in the second floor club room. You're welcome to use the sundeck and handball court on the roof of the nine-story building. You can sleep in a private bedroom in the fraternity house at a charge of $1.25 and up a night.

The fraternity dining room offers a special Anzac lunch every day at 50c. Through Miss Luxford invitations to private homes for dinner are issued to the men. Similar invitations include week-ends in the country with private families at no charge.

The club arranges through the Office of War Information for bi-weekly broadcasts of personal messages from servicemen to their homes in Australia and New Zealand. Sign up at the

Salute to Gallant Donuteers

—who, under great hardships and difficulties, in all degrees of weather, from burning hot to freezing cold . . . at any and every hour of the day or night . . . come through smiling. They bring their trays of heartwarming cheer right up to the advanced combat flying bases, front battle lines, to camps everywhere. To our fighters these donuts are "like a message from home"—give a big boost to morale. They get a joyful, hearty welcome every time.

Visit

The MAYFLOWER Shops

NEW YORK

1531 BROADWAY • 1540 BROADWAY • 11 WEST 42ND STREET

BOSTON • CHICAGO • CINCINNATI • CLEVELAND • DETROIT • HOLLYWOOD
LOS ANGELES • MIAMI • MINNEAPOLIS • OAKLAND • PHILADELPHIA
ROCHESTER • SAN FRANCISCO • WORCESTER • WASHINGTON, D. C.

club-house. Your message will be recorded, shipped to San Francisco, and sent by short-wave to Australia and New Zealand. Your parents will be notified in advance of the broadcast.

HOTEL FOR MERCHANT SEAMEN. The New York Hotel for Merchant Seamen is housed in a seventeen story building at 134 West 58th Street. Here merchant seamen can rent rooms for $1.00 to $2.50. It's open twenty-four hours a day. This residential hotel is operated by the United Seaman's Service, 39 Broadway.

THE RED SHIELD SERVICE MEN'S CLUB, sponsored by the Salvation Army, has its headquarters in the five-story mansion at 12 West 56th Street. The club is open twenty-four hours a day to servicemen of the United Nations.

THE WHITE ENSIGN CLUB has its clubroom on the mezzanine of the Barbizon Plaza Hotel, Sixth Avenue at 58th Street. It is open exclusively to British Royal Navy officers who are required to live at the hotel.

THE OFFICERS' PENTHOUSE CLUB has its headquarters in the penthouse of the Henry Hudson Hotel, 353 West 57th Street. There's a cocktail party every other Thursday afternoon at 6:30 for resident officers. Other men and women officers are welcome to use the clubrooms at any time. It's open twenty-four hours a day.

DEFENSE HOUSE at 50 West 68th Street is a non-sectarian club for soldiers, sailors, marines, and airmen of the United Nations, run by the Women's Division of the American Jewish Congress. The hours are 7 a.m. to 2 a.m. Here you receive a bed at night and a large breakfast in the morning, all for 50c. Phone TRafalgar 4-3331 in advance for a reservation. There are informal parties every Saturday and Sunday afternoon.

A.W.V.S. RECREATION CENTER for service men is open daily from 6 to 11 p.m., Saturdays from 2 p.m. to midnight, Sundays from 2 p.m. to 11 p.m. at 2180 Broadway above the 77th Street Theater. A real home in the big city for visiting service men. Here everyone calls everybody else by their first names, and a man can find all the comforts of home and then some, from shaving and shoe-shine facilities to a mending nook where A.W.V.S. members will sew on buttons and chevrons, mend a torn shirt or darn those hopeless-looking socks.

· THEATERS ·

IN NO OTHER CITY in the world does the theater offer us such a variety of entertainment as in New York. Over 650 play-houses and moving picture theaters are listed. Of these, 72 are in the Broadway district.

Broadway's only links with the past are the Empire at 39th Street and Belasco's at 115 West 44th Street. Both of these houses are in active use. The former, rich in crimson velvet and gilt, caters to social audiences.

* * *

SHUBERT ALLEY. Very much a part of Broadway are Shubert Alley, the Leblang-Gray ticket office and the basement of Walgreen's drugstore.

You'll be near Shubert Alley the night you happen to visit any one of the theaters on 44th or 45th Streets west of Broadway.

The Leblang-Gray ticket office is at 1476 Broadway on the northeast corner of 42nd Street. Don't stop at the main counter. Push your way through to the basement bargains. You may pick up last-minute buys in seats here for half the price you'd pay at box offices, but you can't be choosy.

At Walgreen's, 1501 Broadway, in the Paramount Building, you'll find an unofficial clearing house in the basement for parts among the younger fry. Over 30c lunches ingenues and juveniles swap current agency news.

THE BRASS RAIL ROUTE. In this neighborhood every entrance that is not a theater or stage door leads to a bar. Favorites are Frankie & Johnnie's at 269 West 45th Street, or the Piccadilly Circus Bar in the Piccadilly Hotel at 227 West 45th Street.

Those of the Empire audience who like refreshment with their theater usually go between acts to Schrafft's next door, or after the show drop in at Longchamps on 41st and Broadway for one of George's Frisco Friezes.

WOODSTOCK HOTEL. Across from the Henry Miller Theater at 124 West 43rd Street is one of the best hotels in the theatrical district, the Woodstock. It is a good place to go for refreshment between acts; it is also a good place to remember if you want to stop at a quiet, well-mannered hotel in the theatrical district. Built by Percival Clement, a former Governor of Vermont, it attracts a great many New England and Southern families.

· NIGHT CLUBS ·

NEW YORK at last count had 1275 night clubs. Their development is fairly recent.

Sometime between 1919, the year the Volstead Act was passed, and 1933, the year of repeal, night clubs were born. They were the outgrowth of speakeasies.

Swing Row, the blaring, noisy district which now sprawls its sparkling way along West 52nd Street between 5th and 6th Avenues, came out of this mousy past. Today there are dozens of showy night clubs in this block once noted not for its jazz but for its private homes. Of these present-day clubs the most famous is Jack and Charlie's at 21 West 52nd Street.

* * *

KNOCK BEFORE YOU ENTER. While Twenty One is not a night club in the strict sense of the word, it furnishes entertainment. Soft carpets. Subdued lights. The people you read about. The patrons are the show: Franklin Roosevelt, Jr. ordering a Jack and Charlie special; Clifton Webb at a corner table, Constance and Joan Bennett keeping a date with some movie mogul.

Quite as popular as Twenty One are three other products of the speakeasy era: The Stork Club, the Colony and El Morocco.

The Stork Club is unique. Sherman Billingsley got the idea for the decorations from the polychromatic bow on a customer's hat. In the main dining room, where music is continuous from five in the afternoon until closing at four a.m., mirrors interspersed with gray walls point up the shocking-pink drapes and lemon-yellow ceiling. The adjoining Cub Room, sound proof for conversation, has on its walls portraits by noted artists of their favorite models.

Mr. Billingsley, at the outbreak of the war, started tea dancing to make sure that men on furlough could enjoy every moment of their leave. There is no cover charge for men or women in the services. Luncheon and dinner are à la carte; the average supper check for two would be $15.00, and it is advisable to make reservations.

The white-and-gold Colony at 667 Madison Avenue is not a night club, but it has a fashionably clubby atmosphere and caters to much the same crowd that patronizes El Morocco. Expensive furs. Fabulous jewels. Beautiful women. Society on parade.

Though the Colony Restaurant is not to be confused with the Colony Club, that very social women's organization at 62nd Street and Park Avenue, it is in its way just as exclusive. A small but very beautiful restaurant and steep prices help keep it so.

El Morocco, the exotic night club at 154 East 54th Street, is responsible for the development of that class known as "café society."

As at the Stork Club, an evening at El Morocco, for two, averages about $15.00.

These four places I have spoken of, Twenty One, the Stork Club, the Colony and El Morocco, are the spectacular high spots of New York's night life. There are many others, some perhaps less known, which you may find amusing, for New York has more night clubs than any other city in the world.

LEG SHOWS. But before we try out the little places let me tell you about a few of the big Broadway night clubs: Billy Rose's Diamond Horseshoe, the Hurricane and the Latin Quarter.

The Diamond Horseshoe is at 235 West 46th Street in the Hotel Paramount, downstairs, in what was once the grill. It is an exciting place done in the style and decor of the Diamond Jim Brady era with loads of plush, gilt and red velvet. A girl show is presented twice nightly upon a large stage situated just above and in the back of the bar, which runs the entire length of the room. This gives the male customers a provocative illusion.

Prices are down to earth: Dinners start at $2.50 which is the minimum check.

THE HURRICANE at 1619 Broadway is on the site of the old Paradise restaurant. At the time of this writing, Duke Ellington and his orchestra top the list of entertainers. There's a $2.00 minimum.

THE LATIN QUARTER is at 200 West 48th Street between Broadway and 7th Avenue. It is the former home of the Cotton

Club. There's a $2.00 minimum during the week which mounts to $3.00 on week-ends but the average dinner check ranges between $4.00 and $5.00.

· MOVIE THEATRES ·

MOTION PICTURES were in swaddling clothes when Broadway's first big movie house, the Strand Theatre, opened in 1914.

Today there are about thirty-five moving picture theatres in the Broadway district. They seat more than a quarter of the movie audiences in all the city.

Among the smaller moving picture houses that feature distinctive pictures is the Fifth Avenue Playhouse at 13th Street and 5th Avenue. These movies are chiefly French.

The Little Carnegie at 146 West 57th Street and the 55th Street Playhouse at 154 West 55th Street, also show unusual foreign pictures.

Soviet films are exhibited at the Stanley Theater, 586 Seventh Avenue.

The only Park Avenue theater is the Normandie at 53d Street and Park. It's very modern and very swanky.

· MUSIC ·

THERE ARE TWO REASONS for going to the Metropolitan Opera. The first is to see and hear the opera. The second is to watch the people.

When the Metropolitan Opera House was built in 1883 the 39th Street side was the carriage entrance. It is still the more exclusive approach.

The gallery uses the 40th Street side. This, too, is a spectacle, especially on Saturday night. Some of the people who buy standing room in the gallery have waited since early morning to get tickets. Frequently, at popular operas, the box-office queue will extend from Broadway clear around to 7th Avenue and 40th Street.

Prices range from $5.50 in the orchestra to $1.10 in the top gallery. Special arrangements have been made for service men to attend at greatly reduced rates. Ask about tickets at the U.S.O., Officers Club, or Army and Navy Club.

Backstage, the Metropolitan retains the glamor of the past. The tenors use Caruso's old dressing doom which, before its present coat of paint, had his name on the wall.

THE NEW OPERA COMPANY, one of New York's unique musical institutions, was founded in 1941 by Mrs. Lytle Hull (the former Mrs. Vincent Astor) with a view to giving talented young people an opportunity for operatic experience.

In the fall of 1942 the company turned its attention to the production of light opera to raise funds for financing further grand opera productions. Its Rosalinda, a revival of Johann Strauss' Die Fledermaus, is running at this writing. The company's second light opera production, a revival of The Merry Widow with Jan Kiepura and Marta Eggerth starred, has been one of the two most popular light opera successes offered in New York this season and gives promise of a long run.

Rosalinda is at the Imperial on West 45th Street and The Merry Widow at the Majestic. According to Madame Yolanda Mero-Irion, general manager of the New Opera Company, the Majestic Theatre at 245 West 44th Street will probably be the permanent theater for the new opera company.

CARNEGIE HALL. New Yorkers always associate the Metropolitan with Carnegie Hall, the large, red-brown block of stone

War, Women and Lipstick—

A recent portrait of
Constance Luft Huhn
by Maria de Kammerer

by
CONSTANCE LUFT HUHN
Head of the House of Tangee

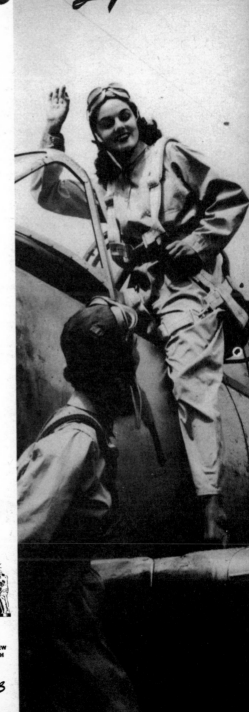

For the first time in history woman-power is a factor in war. Millions of you are fighting and working side by side with your men.

In fact, you are doing double duty—for you are still carrying on your traditional "woman's" work of cooking, and cleaning, and home-making. Yet, somehow, American women are still the loveliest and most spirited in the world. The best dressed, the best informed, the best looking.

It's a reflection of the free democratic way of life that you have succeeded in keeping your femininity—even though you are doing man's work!

If a symbol were needed of this fine, independent spirit—of this courage and strength—I would choose a lipstick. It is one of those mysterious little essentials that have an importance far beyond their size or cost.

A woman's lipstick is an instrument of personal morale that helps her to conceal heartbreak or sorrow; gives her self-confidence when it's badly needed; heightens her loveliness when she wants to look her loveliest.

No lipstick—ours or anyone else's—will win the war. But it symbolizes one of the reasons why we are fighting...the precious right of women to be feminine and lovely—under any circumstances.

The Tangee Satin-Finish Lipstick of your choice will keep your lips smoother...longer! It will bring an exclusive grooming and a deep glowing "life" to your lips that defy both time and weather.

TANGEE
WITH THE NEW
SATIN-FINISH

Lipsticks

at 57th Street and 6th Avenue. To one building they go for their opera, to the other for their symphonic concerts and major recitals.

The hall, built by Andrew Carnegie, is seven years younger than the Metropolitan, but it too has its wealth of tradition.

Here, within its old-fashioned pink walls, have been held the concerts of the New York Symphony, the New York Philharmonic, the Boston Symphony, the Philadelphia Symphony, the New York Oratorical Society. On this stage have appeared most of the great conductors and the great soloists of the world.

The price naturally varies according to the performance. Seats for the Philharmonic are $3.00. Orchestra tickets for a Heifetz concert cost $2.75.

TOWN HALL. Town Hall, however, has never been devoted exclusively, or even primarily, to music. It is owned by the League of Political Education, which was formed in 1894 as an experiment in adult education.

MacDOWELL CLUB. Another organization interested in promoting culture is the MacDowell Club at 166 East 73rd Street. Founded in 1906 in honor of Edward MacDowell, the

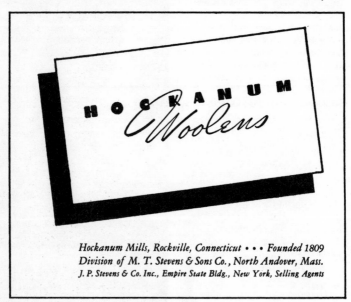

Hockanum Mills, Rockville, Connecticut • • • Founded 1809
Division of M. T. Stevens & Sons Co., North Andover, Mass.
J. P. Stevens & Co. Inc., Empire State Bldg., New York, Selling Agents

• 34 •

composer, it was one of the first groups to recognize the work of the late George Pierce Baker of Harvard.

THE JUILLIARD SCHOOL OF MUSIC. A listing of New York's music centers would not be complete without mention of the Juilliard, at 122nd Street and Claremont Avenue.

The Juilliard School of Music includes three sections: the Juilliard Graduate School, the Institute of Musical Art and the Juilliard Summer School.

The Juilliard Graduate School was organized under the Augustus D. Juilliard Foundation, established in March, 1920. The Graduate School, which became active in 1924, provides free instruction in all branches of music for unusually gifted American and Canadian students who qualify for admission through examinations before the faculty. Its students give over twenty-five concerts and three to four operas each season. Tickets for them are free and may be had by request ahead of time. A series, though, such as the Mozart Festival, costs $5.00.

MUSEUM CONCERTS. David Mannes conducts concerts every year at the Metropolitan Museum of Art. They are held during the month of January.

THE MANNES SCHOOL. The small concert hall of the Mannes School at 157 East 74th Street has the combined quality of a chapel and art gallery. Concerts by students are given here thirty times a year. Admission is by invitation from the students.

GREENWICH HOUSE MUSIC SCHOOL. Concerts are given once a month during the winter in Mrs. Vladimir Simkhovitch's Greenwich House Music School at 46 Barrow Street. Free tickets are obtainable upon request.

ON WITH THE DANCE. You can find every form of dance in New York, from swing to precise, stylized ballet stepping.

If you like to rub elbows with the people there are the two

popular Broadway dance halls, the Arcadia, at Broadway and 53rd Street, and Roseland at 1658 Broadway. These are glorified taxi-dance halls with professional hostesses. Tickets are 11c a dance at Roseland in addition to an admission charge of 75c. At the Arcadia, admission is 65c. Week-end prices are slightly higher.

Dancing of another type is stepped at the Roscommon Club in Tuxedo Hall at 637 Madison Avenue (corner 59th Street), and the Innisfail Ballroom at 200 East 56th Street. Irish jigging is popular here.

Clever, suave and quiet-mannered Arthur Murray runs the town's largest dancing school at 11 East 43rd Street. Lessons come high. Individual instruction costs $2.00 to $2.50 a half hour.

ON THE RECORD. If you want to buy popular dance records I think the Liberty Music Store at 50th and Madison has the best selection.

For foreign tunes and ballads, try the Gramophone Shop at 18 East 48th Street. Many New Yorkers, for some strange reasons, collect sound records. At the Gramophone Shop you can buy anything from a record of the wind howling to the toot of tugboat whistles on a foggy night.

If you don't want to buy records you may listen to your favorite numbers in the Record Booth in a branch of the New York Public Library at 121 East 58th Street.

· BROADCASTING ·

SOLDIERS AND SAILORS have a better chance of getting broadcasting tickets than the general public.

N.B.C. gives a weekly allotment of tickets to the New York City Defense Recreation at 99 Park Avenue, for servicemen, and to the Officers' Service Committee at the Commodore Hotel, for officers.

C.B.S. supplies tickets to men in uniform at their studio building, 49 East 52nd Street. It is open all day and until midnight.

While most New Yorkers would just as soon be caught climbing the Statue of Liberty as seeing a broadcasting station, I think they ought to do both once.

WOR, New York's most popular local station, is at 1440 Broadway.

**TO MAKE A
LOVELY YOU**

Even Lovelier...

He may never know
it was Evening in
Paris face powder that
made him realize he
loves you . . . but he'll
always know you're
thrilling when you're
wearing this face powder
with the enchanting Fra-
grance of Romance.

Evening in Paris FACE POWDER
BOURJOIS

RARELY did a visitor to New York in the early nineteenth century miss seeing Dr. David Hosack's famous Botanical Garden.

Today the only plant life on the site of the doctor's garden is high on the rooftops of Rockefeller Center. But the twelve acres extending from 48th to 51st Streets between 5th and 6th Avenues are still the show place of New York.

Ever since the days of Dr. Hosack, Columbia University has owned this valuable piece of land. In 1929 the Metropolitan Square Corporation leased the property for $3,000,000 a year, Columbia's major source of revenue. The purpose of the corporation, backed by John D. Rockefeller, Jr. was to erect a new opera house. When plans fell through, Mr. Rockefeller decided to go ahead and build anyway. His pioneer tenants were the Radio Corporation of America, the National Broadcasting Company and the Radio-Keith-Orpheum Corporation.

The Time & Life Building was completed in 1937 and the Associated Press building followed. The Eastern Airlines Building, embracing Holland House, the Dutch headquarters, was one of the later constructions. The United States Rubber Company Building on Sixth Avenue was opened last.

There are guided tours every half hour which for $1.10 give a fairly comprehensive idea of the general setup. They start at Concourse 4 of the R.C.A. Building and take you from the warehouse, seven feet below sea level, all the way to the R.C.A. Observation Roof, 850 feet high.

The presence of the consulates in the Center adds a foreign flavor to all the buildings, which is carried even underground. All these foreign tenants make use of the bonded warehouse which the Center maintains in the subbasement. It is a "free port," which means that any store in the Center can import goods, place them in the warehouse and then borrow them for exhibition purposes. If a sale occurs duty must be paid, but if there is no sale the store can return the goods without paying duty. A special law called the Rockefeller Center Exhibition Act was passed by Congress to make this warehouse possible.

The Center Post Office, which brings in $1.00 annual rent from the federal government, also serves tenants. It is located in the north Concourse of the R.C.A. Building.

Nearby is Charles De Zemler's Barber Shop, one of the most fascinating shops in the Center. Mr. De Zemler, a Swede by birth, is a man imbued with a keen appreciation of the tradition of his profession. He has been collecting tonsorialana for the past twenty years and likes to show off his rarer and more interesting pieces.

While still in the gadget-gazing mood you must pay a visit to the Museum of Science and Industry in the R.C.A. Building. It's one of those rare museums where "Do Not Touch" signs have never been heard of. You are urged to press buttons, pull levers and see for yourself what happens behind the scenes of the very latest scientific discoveries.

The museum is open every day from 10 a.m. to 10 p.m. Admission is 28c for adults and 11c for children.

After an hour or more in the museum your appetite will be sufficiently whetted to do justice to lunch on the Lower Plaza. There are two restaurants to choose from, the English Grill and the Restaurant Francais, each, of course, specializing in native dishes. Luncheons start at $1.25.

In the summer meals are served outdoors under gay colored umbrellas to the tune of the splashing water of the Prometheus fountain. In the winter the entire Lower Plaza is transformed into an outdoor artificial ice-skating pond. As you eat snug and warm indoors, you can watch the skating outside.

Formal gardens with wide lawns bordered by hedges and flower beds adorn the roof of the British Empire Building. When you look toward St. Patrick's it seems as if the spires were rising directly from the green lawns in front of you. Only the tops of other buildings in the vicinity prevent you from thinking you're in some English cathedral close.

There are three theaters in Rockefeller Center, the Center Theater, the Radio City Music Hall and the Newsreel Theater. The Center Theater seats 3700. The Music Hall, seating 6200, is the largest theater in the world. It is used principally for motion pictures. The Newsreel shows the news of the world and selected short subjects in a one hour show.

REILLY'S HEALTH SERVICE in the R.C.A. Building at Rockefeller Center is just what the name implies. It is a superlative sunlight gymnasium with ultra-violet ceiling radiation which specializes in Electric Galvanic, Effervescent Pine, Tonic Spray, Oxygen, Alkaline, Sitz, Foam, Nauheim and Heller Baths, as well as electric cabinets, steam and vapor baths; special Dierker Scientific Colonics; reducing and passive reducing.

H. J. Reilly, the health service head, is a wizard when it comes to keeping the human body in condition. Among his satisfied clients are the Duke and Duchess of Windsor, Ganna Walska, General J. G. Harbord, David Sarnoff and hundreds of other famous people.

• CANTEENS •

THE ENGLISH SPEAKING UNION at 30 Rockefeller Plaza serves tea for officers every afternoon. Open house Sunday evening. This means a snack, music and entertainment.

There is a dinner dance each Wednesday night. Notice must be given ahead of time for the dinner dances and men must come stag as girls are invited by the English Speaking Union. Everything is free. For officers only.

*　*　*

THE MAPLE LEAF SNACK BAR (CANADIAN) at 601 Fifth Avenue is open from 8 a.m. to 8 p.m. A club for service men of the Allied Armies and Navies and men of the Merchant Marine, it offers refreshments, lounge, books and magazines.

NATIONAL CATHOLIC COMMUNITY SERVICE while not in Rockefeller Center, should be included in this chapter, because it is just a block away at 17 East 51st Street, across from St. Patrick's.

Servicemen and women of this country and our Allies are welcome. The Canteen offers them free meals between 12 noon and 8 p.m.

THE VILLAGE is a great place to buy knick-knacks. Here you can collect anything from batik-patterned silk to hand-wrought silver.

The streets have such a way of crisscrossing one another, that even the Villagers can't find their own keyholes. For a locality that is so easy to reach, Greenwich Village is the most difficult place in New York to find your way about. It straggles south of 14th Street across from Fifth Avenue to the Hudson River by way of devious streets.

The Independent subway or the Fifth Avenue bus are the simplest means of transit. Get off at Washington Square on the subway or 8th Street on the bus.

FRED LEIGHTON'S LA FIESTA INDIAN TRADING POST at 15 East 8th Street is a little shop that deals exclusively in Indian-made handcrafts. It carries pottery, blankets, Navajo rugs, moccasins and Guatemalan dolls. The Mexican glass is very lovely.

BREVOORT AND LAFAYETTE HOTELS. For many years they have been two popular spots in town. They still retain their charm. The cooking is French.

The Brevoort at Fifth Avenue and 8th Street was the first hotel in New York to have a sidewalk cafe.

The Lafayette is on the corner of 9th Street and University Place. It is the site of the old Café Martin, frequented by every celebrity of the social and artistic world of New York. Visit the checker room.

THE BAMBOO FOREST at 27 West 8th Street. This is a little restaurant where you can get a very good Chinese dinner for 65c. Noodles, shrimp and pineapple salad and jasmine tea are their specialties.

As for Village Night Clubs:

JIMMY KELLY'S at 181 Sullivan Street, is cheerful and noisy. There's dancing and a floor show. The place always makes me think of a movie version of an old-fashioned Western dance hall. Five dollars will cover dinner for two. Cocktails extra.

EL CHICO is a Spanish cabaret at 80 Grove Street. The music is loud but the atmosphere is Latin.

ASTI'S at 79 West 12th Street just off Sixth Avenue, although not strictly a night club, should be mentioned here. It captures the carefree spirit of the old Greenwich Village. Here you will dine to the score of Figaro or Rigoletto. Everyone sings, from the guests to the waiters and bartenders. The five-course Italian dinner, served from 6 to 9:30, will cost you $1.50.

CAFE SOCIETY DOWNTOWN for boogie-woogie fans. There are three shows every night except Monday in this lively spot at 2 Sheridan Square. An average dinner costs $2.50.

CHARLES at Sixth Avenue and 11th Street. Another typically French place in the Village. The restaurant is famed for its pot au feu (boiled chicken dinner) and lobster á la Newburg, a creamy rich dish, and also for its home-made pastry. An average dinner costs $2.50.

HISTORY OF THE NEIGHBORHOOD. Greenwich Village, as far as the artists and writers are concerned, started on Washington Square.

The art and literary colony which made the Village famous lived in New York University on the east side of the square.

Among the first to engage quarters were Brander Matthews, Mark Twain, William Dean Howell, Henry James and F. Hopkinson Smith. Not all could find lodgings in the University, and so some took rooms in houses round about and thus began the history of Greenwich Village as a literary and artistic colony.

GOING HOME

This is Flight 44. It shortens the distance between places by many hours. It makes possible a trip for busy people who otherwise would not have time to go.

Like this boy in uniform—going home. Going home, on a furlough for just 30 hours. Going home, to a piece of Mother's apple pie . . . a few hours with Mary . . . a heart-to-heart talk with Dad. Going home, to sleep in his own bed . . . to take a long look at everything he cares about.

He thinks about these things now . . . and he thinks about the man who, ten minutes ago, gave up his seat in the plane to him. He remembers that the man looked important, and busy. But the man overheard him say he couldn't get home at all in 30 hours unless he got on this plane. And the man had stepped up and asked to be changed to a later flight . . . and he had said something about a responsibility to men in uniform. And something about . . . one of the reasons we have an America to fight for is because Americans take time to think about the other fellow.

The boy felt warm and good inside. A stranger knew how much it meant to a soldier to be going home. Going home . . . maybe for the last time in a long while. Maybe for the last time.

To our boys in the Armed Forces, leave is the most precious thing they can have. Maybe they're only coming home from camp. Maybe they're coming back from the hellholes of the Solomons or Africa. Every hour, every minute of that leave means more to them than they can say. For many of them, with the little time they have, the only way they can get home, the only way they can see their folks again, is to fly. We of Eastern Air Lines would like to give each one of them an "unofficial priority." But we can't. So we're going to leave it up to you—and we don't mean that you should stop traveling by air for the duration. Just continue to make plane reservations—and if your business is important or your trip is urgent, travel as usual. However, if you find you can take a later plane and there's a soldier, sailor or marine waiting—who can't get home and back in time any other way—why not give him your seat?

Eddie Rickenbacker

President and General Manager
EASTERN *Air Lines*

EASTERN
Air Lines

WASHINGTON SQUARE, NORTH. The delightful old red-brick and white-trimmed houses have graced the north side of the Square for a century. The row occupying the block from University Place to Fifth Avenue, belongs to Sailors Snug Harbor, a corporation that now controls more than fifty million dollars' worth of New York real estate.

It is all part of the original Randall farm, left more than a hundred years ago as a source of income for clipper-ship and steamboat sailors no longer able to work.

The potter's field (now Washington Square) which edged the south side of Captain Randall's farm, had been leveled in 1823. Washington Square was opened in 1827.

The north side of Washington Square is still an aristocratic residential locality. The stables back of it have been converted into studios. The row is called Washington Mews. One of its residents is Grover Whalen.

STREET FAIR. Village artists hold an outdoor painting exhibit each spring and fall. It begins at 8th and MacDougal Streets and trails down MacDougal to 3rd Street, curves round Washington Square South and branches off, along the way, into separate miniature shows. The exhibition is amusing whether the pictures are good or bad.

You may like to know that among other things in the Village is the:

NEW SCHOOL FOR SOCIAL RESEARCH at 66 West 12th Street. The cubistic-looking building is maintained for advanced adult education.

The neighborhood house of the section is run by Mrs. V. G. Simkhovitch at 27 Barrow Street and is called

GREENWICH HOUSE. You will find it intensely interesting, particularly the pottery.

Connected with past history is the first studio building to be erected in New York at 51 West 10th Street.

· 44 ·

SALMAGUNDI CLUB at 47 Fifth Avenue, the dignified meeting place of older artists, is another famous spot.

On the southeast corner of Fifth Avenue and 9th Street at Number 21 is the house in which Mark Twain used to live. It has been converted into small kitchenette apartments.

Greenwich Village itself was a self-sufficient town, up to the middle part of the nineteenth century, separated by fields and woods from New York proper.

The Sullivan Street gardens are also quite picturesque. Everybody in the Village knows the house where Edna Saint Vincent Millay once lived on Cherry Lane between Bedford Street and the Cherry Lane Theater. A black iron gate opens upon the trim little lawn and fresh bushes that guard it.

The tower of Jefferson Market Court has cast its shadow across Greenwich Avenue many years. Next to it rises the women's prison. Patchin Place is just across the street, a delightful little three-cornered nook lighted by an old street lamp and bordered by quaint houses.

A.W.V.S. UNIT. 52 East 9th Street. In an old brownstone house where once lived Lillian Russell, toast of the gay nineties and friend of Diamond Jim Brady, the members of the A.W.V.S. Greenwich Village Unit now make their headquarters.

And if you have some shopping to do, you might stop in at the unit's Bargain Shop, 121 Seventh Avenue. Perhaps you'll find a gift that appeals to you for some one at home, and the amount of your purchase will be used to further the work of the unit.

MUSIC BOX CANTEEN at 68 Fifth Avenue, is open every day from three in the afternoon until 12 at night. Servicemen and women as well as merchant seamen are invited.

· OLD CHELSEA ·

CHELSEA is one of the sections which has changed least. The most picturesque portion is around the General Theological Seminary at 9th Avenue and 20th Street. The two families who contributed opulence and dignity to its fame were the Moores and the Cushmans.

Dr. Clement C. Moore taught at the Seminary from 1821 to 1850. He interrupted his scholarly pursuits to shush his grandchildren with a jingle called "The Night Before Christmas." His Hebrew-English Lexicon in two volumes has long since been forgotten but his nursery rhyme is known round the world.

St. Peter's at 346 West 20th Street, is called "The Night Before Christmas Church" because Dr. Moore played the organ there.

The present London Terrace, rated as one of the city's largest apartment houses with its 1500 tenants, is built on ground once graced by a row of colonnaded houses, homes of the society leaders.   *   *   *

A.W.V.S. LONDON TERRACE UNIT. The 400 members of this active A.W.V.S. group are all residents of London Terrace, which stretches the entire length of the block from 9th to 10th Avenues and from 23rd to 24th Streets. The A.W.V.S. unit makes its headquarters in the attractive Penthouse Club at 470 West 24th Street, which incidentally, commands a magnificent view of the Hudson River.

The unit's Thrift Shop, 199 Ninth Avenue, is by way of becoming a neighborhood institution. All articles sold here are donated and among them are some outstanding items.

A.W.V.S. CHELSEA UNIT. In an old store at 277 Eighth Avenue is the headquarters of the Chelsea Unit of the A.W.V.S.

THE HUDSON GUILD NEIGHBORHOOD HOUSE at 436 West 27th Street holds open house on Wednesday and Friday nights for Coast Guard boys in the neighborhood. Dancing and games are followed by coffee and cake.

Old Chelsea touches the waterfront. Along 12th Avenue from 23rd Street to 14th Street, you find a hodge-podge of tiny shops wedged in between sailors' pool-halls and one-arm lunch rooms. Some of the stores are Spanish and Portuguese. Before the war you could pick up amusing bargains in perfume, soaps and cheap foreign souvenirs.

Chelsea has many sides. The gray stone, ivy-covered buildings of the General Theological Seminary remind you of England.

The ancient, balcony-trimmed Chelsea Hotel at 222 West 23rd Street suggests a Victorian dowager. Cavanagh's at 258 West 23rd Street, the best restaurant in Chelsea (it has been there half a century), is reminiscent of coaching days.

FOR SEAMEN. The Seamen's House Y.M.C.A. at 550 West 20th Street (corner of 11th Avenue) is open day and night for merchant seamen. To get here take a 14th Street crosstown bus marked West 22nd Street Ferry, and get off at 20th Street and 11th Avenue. You pay 50c for a bed in the dormitory, 85c to $1.25 for a private room.

Merchant seamen may receive dental service at a nominal

cost, thanks to the American Women's Hospitals Reserve Corps. Women dentists from the corps do the work on Tuesdays and Fridays by appointment. Call WAtkins 9-1045.

· *LITTLE FRANCE* ·

THIS SECTION extends from 30th Street south to 26th Street west of 8th Avenue.

FRENCH RESTAURANTS. Here is a list of all-French restaurants given me by a Frenchman who knows good food—but what Frenchman doesn't?

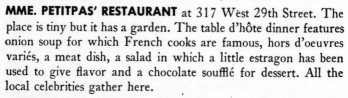

   *The Cafe Chambord, 803 Third Avenue.
   *La Chaumiere, 163 East 56th Street.
   Maurice Raviol, 3 East 48th Street.
   L'Aiglon, 13 East 55th Street.
   L'Auberge, 58 West 56th Street.
   *Fleur de Lis, 141 West 69th Street.
   *Couret, 11 West 56th Street.
   Pinguin, 351 West 57th Street.
   I have starred those which I have sampled more than once.

MME. PETITPAS' RESTAURANT at 317 West 29th Street. The place is tiny but it has a garden. The table d'hôte dinner features onion soup for which French cooks are famous, hors d'oeuvres variés, a meat dish, a salad in which a little estragon has been used to give flavor and a chocolate soufflé for dessert. All the local celebrities gather here.

LITTLE FRANCE GOES TO CHURCH. St. Vincent de Paul is the oldest French house of worship in New York. It was built long before the French people in this country thought of settling in the district where they now live. It stands at 127 West 23rd Street. French weddings are often held in the chapel.

Down on lower Sixth Avenue at 124 West 16th Street, is a quaint old-fashioned building with a curious courtyard that shelters the French Young Women's Christian Union. The building has been there many years. It suggests a convent.

The Comte Charles de Fontnouvelle, former French Consul General in New York, heads the Lycee Francais at 3 East 95th

Street, our city's most popular foreign school. The pupils represent seventeen different nationalities.

Papa Pernot's shop at 484 Tenth Avenue is the favorite delicatessen of the French. It specializes in paties and cheeses.

The favorite French drugstore is LeGoll's Pharmacy at 581 Tenth Avenue. It carries a complete line of French drugs.

· SPAIN ·

AN OCCASIONAL RESTAURANT or shop and a scattering of dark-eyed people on Cherry Street is all that's left of old Spain. The hub of the Latin-American section in New York is in the over-congested district which extends from 110th Street north to 125th Street, east to Lexington Avenue and west to 8th Avenue.

* * *

JAI ALAI. You can get Spanish rice or Baela a la Valenciana, as it's sometimes called, in the Jai Alai, a little Spanish restaurant at 82 Bank Street. When you go, order membrillo (preserved quinces) and cream cheese for dessert.

Among the Spanish restaurants in addition to Jai Alai are La Bilbaina at 218 West 14th Street, Fornos at 236 West 52nd Street, and El Chico at 80 Grove Street.

FOODSTUFFS. I often buy guava jelly in Moneo's tiny Spanish delicatessen store at 218 West 14th Street.

For preserved guavas I go to the Victori Co. at 164 Pearl Street. If you like chocolate bars, this is a good place to get them. They are very sweet and flavored with cinnamon. A large cake costs 30c.

A.W.V.S. SPANISH UNIT. 174 East 110th Street. Up on the balcony of the Aquillar Branch of the New York Public Library, appropriately surrounded by Spanish books and magazines, is the headquarters of the A.W.V.S. Spanish Unit. It has a Recreation Center for Service Men in the old ball room above the Casa Gonzales store at 170 East 116th Street.

· *IRELAND* ·

THE IRISH, once a very dominant and friendly influence in New York, no longer congregate in any one neighborhood. Here and there you may see an Irish name above a shop, but they are few and far between. One of the most interesting is The All Ireland Music Store at 1456 Third Avenue, which sells Irish music, jigs and songs, and Irish knick-knacks. Another is the Irish Industries Depot at 876 Lexington Avenue. They handle Irish china, tweeds, poplin ties, linen handkerchiefs and books.

The Irish Echo, a newspaper published at 152 East 121st Street, is a nucleus for a loyal little group of Irish folk, some of whom live opposite in a quaint row of houses known as Sylvan Court.

The Tuxedo ballroom at 59th Street and Madison Avenue, and the Innisfail at 200 East 56th Street, are the only real Irish dance halls left in New York.

You'll still find some of the fighting Irish in Hell's Kitchen, which runs from 8th to 12th Avenues between 38th and 52nd Streets.

Hell's Kitchen laps over on San Juan Hill, once quite as notorious as the former locality for lawless characters.

San Juan Hill, which extends from 52nd to 59th Street west of 9th Avenue, was named during the Spanish American War. It includes Roosevelt Hospital.

*   *   *

BAR AND GRILL. Jack Delaney's at 72 Grove Street, should also be mentioned here. It's a favorite restaurant among the Villagers, and deservedly so. Good food is Jack's specialty.

A.W.V.S. IN LITTLE IRELAND. One of the largest and busiest A.W.V.S. units in Manhattan, with more than four thousand registered members, the A.W.V.S. 9th Division makes its headquarters at 15 West 44th Street but includes Little Ireland in its broad territory.

The unit also runs a salvage depot at 11 East 47th Street from which regular collections in a gaily painted pushcart are made as far West as Hell's Kitchen. And last but not least, members of the Division staff the popular Outdoor Library in Bryant Park during the summer. This outdoor library, by the way, is a unique and delightful New York institution, a wonderful place to relax between your sightseeing jaunts, and it goes without saying that service men and women are especially welcome.

· $\mathcal{N}$EWSPAPER ROW ·

THIS used to be the name for Park Row in the blocks between Chambers and William Streets. The Sun was at 170 Nassau, the Times at 113 Nassau, the Tribune at 41 Park Row and the New York World at 63 Park Row.

Today there is not a single newspaper office on Park Row though three still remain in the vicinity; the Journal-American at 210 South Street, the New York Sun at 280 Broadway, the Post at 75 West Street and my paper, the World-Telegram at 125 Barclay Street. The Herald Tribune is now located at 230 West 41st Street and the Times at 229 West 43rd Street.

My favorite downtown French restaurant, André's, is at 3 Frankfort Street opposite the World Building. André's is run by a chef and three waiters from Old Mouquin's. You'll find such delicacies as Oysters a la Rockefeller and Green

Turtle Soup on the menu. Luncheon is the main meal. It costs about one dollar per person.

TANNERS' ROW is further down on Frankfort Street. In the great arches beneath Brooklyn Bridge are the tanners of New York City. The men who deal in raw hides and pelts have congregated in the quaint warehouses that line Gold Street from the time Brooklyn Bridge was built. Even before the bridge loomed up they did business at the same stand. Theirs is one of the few industries which the march of progress has not affected, from Colonial times down to the present.

* * *

THE GILDED DOME of the old Pulitzer Building was right in the midst of things for a great many years—and still is. To the north is the Municipal Building, where the marriage licenses may be purchased. A few steps farther up at 27 Duane Street is St. Andrews, the printers' church. The Reverend William E. Cashin, confessor at Sing-Sing for twenty-five years as well as father confessor at the Tombs, is the rector. A jolly, round-faced, big-hearted Irishman, he probably knows the solution of more murders, hold-ups and crime tales than any other man living. Being chief confessor at Sing-Sing and the Tombs brings its share of tragic knowledge.

St. Andrew's got its subtitle from the fact that every morning at two o'clock a mass was held for the reporters and printers who work on the lobster shift of the daily papers.

Across from the World Building is City Hall, a structure that to me is one of the loveliest in New York. The interior is Colonial. The center hall with its spiral staircase, and the high-ceilinged, paneled rooms where the Mayor of the City of New York has his offices, are perfect examples of the period.

· *LITTLE TURKEY* ·

WASHINGTON STREET from Battery Place to Fulton Street, is known as Little Turkey. Here you may buy rose-water and brassware, including the very attractive little individual brass coffee-pots used in Constantinople, foreign silk-stuffs and a vast amount of Oriental embroidery.

THE SON OF THE SHEIK at 77 Washington Street serves lamb in grape leaves and cooked on a spit. All the restaurants in this neighborhood have pilaff of rice on the table and honey and rose-water pastry.

Noon is the best time to try these places. Nine o'clock will find lights out and pavements deserted.

SWEETMEATS. You'll find the Syrian shops clustered round the beginning of Washington Street.

Nicholas Abaid, at 53 Washington Street, makes delicious apricot paste and Turkish halva. Mr. Abaid, a native of Damascus, runs his candy factory in the shop. His father and mother, grandfather and grandmother were Syrian confectioners. The Damascus sweetmeats he makes and sells have helped put his five children through high school and college.

The Armenians are slow to give up the customs of their own land. Still dear to their hearts are the ceremonies that surround every death. At a funeral on Washington Street, you may see the women veiled in white cloth, seated about the casket. They rock back and forth moaning until the corpse has been carried out. The room in which the body lies is also completely draped in white.

The few down-at-the-heels Colonial houses that linger on the street tell of its once fashionable history. The close of the Civil War marked a change in the narrow thorofare. Some think that the proximity of Castle Garden in the days when it was serving as a landing-place for the emigrants had a great deal to do with the sudden influx of foreigners to the once beautiful old section. 1889 saw the height of foreign emigration pouring in through this channel.

When the war is over Little Turkey will be wiped out. The new tunnel to Brooklyn is going to cut in here.

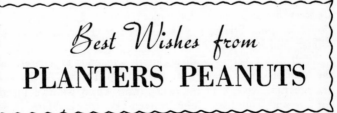

A.W.V.S. DOWNTOWN UNIT. Not far from the heart of Little Turkey, in the old convent at Barclay and Church Streets, is Saint Peter's School. If you were to drop in between the hours of 7 and 10 some fall or winter evening, you would find a group of A.W.V.S. members, volunteers from the organization's Downtown Unit, surrounded by eager children and young people ranging in age from four-year olds to high school seniors, all from the district known as Little Turkey.

A.W.V.S. MOTOR TRANSPORT SERVICE. Walking through this section of the city you are bound to come upon the huge office building at 90 Church Street, now being used as administrative headquarters by various branches of the United States Navy. There you will see a special parking lot assigned to the volunteer drivers of the A.W.V.S. Motor Transport Service.

· *FINANCIAL NEW YORK* ·

IN THE FINANCIAL DISTRICT you may be surprised to find layer upon layer of romance. Go there frequently with your eyes open. You'll see a bit of the Latin Quarter above an old restaurant called Oscar's Old Delmonico at 56 Beaver Street which once belonged to the original Delmonico. There, on the top floor of what appears to be a matter-of-fact office building, are a series of picturesque studios overlooking New York Harbor.

One time while on a story I came across the old frame house at Number 7 Peck Slip where Mr. D. T. Valentine, the first person to write consistently of New York, passed his youth.

On still another occasion I took tea in a delightful 18th Century house I had never noticed before. The only private home on John Street, it was occupied by Howard Baer, the painter, and his wife.

Wall Street begins with a church and ends in a river. At the head of it rises the slender spire of old Trinity. At the foot are the East River and the docks from which we used to sail for tropical countries. The canyon-like thoroughfare is so named because the north end of the stockade built by the Dutch in the early 17th century formed a wall. The Dutch expected an attack from Connecticut. Their stockade followed the direction taken by the dark, narrow little street now overshadowed by huge buildings.

The best way to see Wall Street is to walk from Broadway straight across to South Street, its eastern boundary.

At Broad and Exchange Place is the Sub-Treasury Building on the site of Federal Hall where George Washington took his oath as first President of the United States.

Across the way at 23 Wall Street is the great banking house of J. P. Morgan and Company. The interior makes you think of some fine, old British Club—good but worn leather chairs, high ceilings and expensively conservative decorations.

From the corner where the Morgan banking house stands you can look down Broad Street to Fraunces Tavern, the Colonial Inn at 54 Pearl Street, where Washington made his farewell speech to his officers.

This building has been restored by the Sons of the American Revolution. There is a good restaurant.

Although Wall Street has never entirely recovered from the '29 crash, business is still active enough. The place where most of it is transacted is the Stock Exchange. While civilians are permitted in the galleries of the Stock and Curb Exchanges when introduced personally by a member, men in uniform are admitted without any formality. Visiting hours are from ten to three on weekdays and from ten to twelve on Saturdays.

Famous buildings pierce the skyline of financial New York. The Equitable Building at 120 Broadway is the city's most valuable property. It was assessed at $28,750,000 in 1942. The National Distillers, one of this book's sponsors, has its headquarters in the Equitable Building.

On the other side of the street is the Singer Building at 149 Broadway, once the world's highest skyscraper. It antedated as the world's tallest building both the Metropolitan Life Tower and the Woolworth Building.

Another famous building in Lower New York is 26 Broadway, the home of Standard Oil. Originally built by the Standard Oil Company of New York in 1885, it has remained in the hands of that company ever since.

The building stands in a part of New York that is inseparably linked with the history of the city and the nation. It faces Bowling Green and it was on Bowling Green that Peter Minuit bought New York from the Indians. Bowling Green is a little patch of green now, but it was much larger in those primitive and remote days when the Dutch settlers called it the Plaine and the Marchveldt and herded their cattle on it. On the other side of Broadway, across Bowling Green, the Dutch built New Amsterdam's first house.

Where the Custom House now stands, there was once Fort Amsterdam, the first fort thrown up in what is now Manhattan.

Marketfield Street is that tiny thoroughfare which curves from Beaver through to Broad.

Facing the small square where the Dutch women once congregated for market-day, is the red-brick building that houses the New York Produce Exchange. It was erected in 1881 on the site of the First French Huguenot Church in New York. Little goes on there these days. They will escort service men through the building from ten to three.

At the end of Marketfield Street (it is not even half a block long) has been placed a bronze tablet which marks the beginning of a forgotten thoroughfare—Petticoat Lane, one of the oldest streets in New York, which started at this point and extended past the fort to what is now Battery Place.

If you follow Wall Street east you will come to India House on Hanover Square. Nearby is the historic New York Coffee and Sugar Exchange where trading has been suspended because of the war.

The official address of the old Exchange is 113 Pearl Street, a thoroughfare that in George Washington's day was the most fashionable street in New York. It gets its name from the pearl shells found in this locality by the Dutch.

Chophouses are tucked in devious side-alleys which lead off Wall Street, relics of a day when foaming ale, a thick juicy chop wrapped about a good fat kidney and broiled to a rich brown, formed the substantial luncheon of New York business men.

Farrish's Chop House at 42 John Street, has been serving steaks and chops to Wall Street brokers since 1856. The pleasant leisurely quality of old New York is reflected in the comfortable proportions, easy-going waiters, wide wooden tables and home cooking. Dickens and Thackeray might have found it to their liking.

In Ye Olde Chop House at 118 Cedar Street, you step back a century when you cross the threshold. One hundred years have seen little change in the place.

There is the same carefully scrubbed wooden floor, strewn with sawdust, the long bar, the little stalls with small bare tables and the wide smoke-darkened beams hung with great copper pots and pans.

Most of the restaurants around Wall Street are only for luncheon. The silence of the grave descends on the district after 6 o'clock.

SEAMEN'S CHURCH INSTITUTE. The Seamen's Church Institute of New York at 25 South Street, is the largest shore home in the world for merchant seamen and officers. Dating back to 1834, it caters to all races and creeds. Between six and eight thousand men frequent the building daily.

The Conrad Library contains 9,000 volumes of all types, but specializes in marine technical books. Ask the registrar about the school for seamen who wish to study for higher ratings. You attend classes on the roof where there's a model pilot house and flying bridge.

A.W.V.S. CANTEEN CORPS. At 11 Broadway on a Sunday noon or evening, you are likely to encounter the A.W.V.S. Canteen Corps at work. Their functions being to serve refreshments to the service men from local camps who are being shown New York for the first time.

A.W.V.S. DOWNTOWN UNIT. The headquarters are in Room 3163 of the Equitable Building at 120 Broadway. In the Chamber of Commerce Building at 59 Liberty Street, at 120 Broadway and at 149 Broadway, you will find A.W.V.S. members taking civilian fingerprints for the city's War Identification Bureau, and at 2 Rector Street you may see a canteen course in session.

CAMERAS. If you are a dyed-in-the-wool camera fan, make a bee-line for Haber and Fink's store at 12 Warren Street. It is between Broadway and Church, just a few blocks north of the Woolworth Building.

Ask for Harry Haber. He knows all the answers when it comes to taking better pictures. You will have to fight your way through the crowd of eager lens hounds which always surrounds him. I'm one of them.

EQUITABLE BUILDING

ERECTED on the site of the greatest fire in New York's history, The Equitable Building is in the heart of New York's famous financial district. Nearby are such other noteworthy buildings as the Stock Exchange, the Sub-Treasury, Trinity Church, and the House of Morgan.

The "resident population" of this building includes 12,000 persons—among whom are the men and women who comprise the "home office" of National Distillers Products Corporation.

NATIONAL DISTILLERS PRODUCTS CORPORATION

120 BROADWAY, NEW YORK 5, N. Y.

ONE MILLION AND FORTY THOUSAND Italians live in the five boroughs. They are scattered in settlements throughout Manhattan, the Bronx, Brooklyn and Staten Island.

Although the largest Italian settlement is in Harlem, the red wine and plaster-saint district just above Chinatown is not without charm. In this section along Elizabeth and Mulberry Streets the shops, restaurants and places of amusement are purely Italian. One hears but little English.

This down-town Little Italy is the oldest Italian settlement in New York. Its boundary-lines are Mulberry, Baxter, Lafayette, 14th Streets and the East River.

Closely linked with its history is St. Patrick's Old Cathedral at 272 Mulberry Street. Visit the church if history appeals to you. Stephen Jumel is buried here. Those who like old epitaphs will find the wall-enclosed burying-ground at the side and back of the church absorbing. The inscriptions tell much of early New York. Ten thousand Italians live in the parish of St. Patrick's. Every priest speaks their language.

Up another block at 304 Mulberry Street stands a quaint, old-fashioned Colonial red-brick house made distinctive by a wide-open, hospitable-looking friendly white door. The building is St. Barnabas House, the place that gives shelter to women and children in need, night or day, with no questions asked.

Charles Dickens made his home on Lafayette Street when he came to New York. The building in which he lived is now Conte's Restaurant and Apartments. The address is 432 Lafayette.   *   *   *

A.W.V.S. IN LITTLE ITALY. New York has many Little Italies and most New York City Italians are intensely loyal to their adopted country. In the uptown section over near the East River between 104th and 121st Streets, the A.W.V.S. Spanish Unit has many projects which include their Italian-speaking neighbors.

Downtown in the Mulberry Street district, the A.W.V.S. Knickerbocker Village Unit at 42 Monroe Street faces the Italian St. Joseph's Church and a row of houses inhabited largely by families of Sicilian descent.

In the heart of New York's Chinatown

· CHINATOWN ·

CHINATOWN abounds in chop-suey restaurants and curio shops. The eating houses are exactly alike as far as exterior decorations go. The same white-tiled entranceways, teakwood mother-of-pearl topped tables and cane-seated Grand Rapids chairs.

But there is a difference in the food. The best of the lot, the Port Arthur, is one flight up at 7 Mott Street. The chow mein is delicious and reasonable, 50c a portion. Quite as appetizing are the little almond meal cakes served with preserved ginger. I recommend also the jasmine tea.

Chinatown covers a small area. The principal streets are Mott, Doyers and Pell.

Not until a few years before the Civil War, however, did Orientals appear in the vicinity. I am told that the first Chinese in New York was a native of Canton, Ah Ken, a cigar dealer who lived on Mott Street. By 1890 there were one thousand Chinese in his neighborhood. The late '90s saw the heyday of the district.

Today it is still a fascinating though passive shadow of its former somewhat lurid self. The people are friendly, the shops intriguing and the atmosphere that of a quaint gas-light New York.

One of the main points of interest is the bulletin board at Mott and Doyers Streets which marks the division of the Hip Song and On Leon Tongs, where the people of the neighborhood gather to read the war news. Tong wars have been forgotten in the common bond of a greater war.

A.W.V.S. CHINESE UNIT. In the annex to the historic Chinese School in the heart of Chinatown at 64 Mott Street, there is an Information and Hospitality Center for Service Men conducted under the joint auspices of the A.W.V.S. Chinese Unit and members of the Chinese Women's New Life Movement, an international organization founded by China's beloved first lady, Madame Chiang Kai Shek. For service men who want to know where to go in this picturesque and interesting part of the city, charming Chinese girls, some in the trim uniform of the A.W.V.S., some in the native dress of the Dragon Land, are on hand every afternoon from two to five to answer questions.

· THE BOWERY ·

THE BOWERY is a legend.

Its shabby length is shrouded in memories of a more lurid past. From its beginning at Chatham Square to its end at Cooper Square, this section of Third Avenue is nothing but a series of dilapidated old buildings, disinfectant-perfumed flop houses, cheap lunch rooms and dingy saloons.

Gone is the famous Five Points Mission; Diamond Lil and her golden swan bed; Joe McGurk's Suicide Hall; the Thalia Opera House and Nigger Mike's.

The only interesting section of the Bowery today is a small stretch which extends from Doyers to Canal Streets under the Third Avenue El. Here you will find some of the color of other days.

Among Our Sponsors

Members of the METROPOLITAN BREWERS' INSTITUTE
and the BREWERS' BOARD OF TRADE, INC.:

P. BALLANTINE & SONS   PETER DOELGER BREWING CORP.

BURKE BREWERY, INC.   CHRISTIAN FIEGANSPAN BREWING CO.

EDELBRAU BREWERY, INC   THE JACOB HOFFMAN BREWING CO.

HOFFMAN BEVERAGE CO.   NORTH AMERICAN BREWING CO.

KIPS BAY BREWING CO.   RUBSAM & HORRMANN BREWING CO.

LINDEN BREWERY, INC.   THE F. & M. SCHAEFER BREWING CO.

PIEL BROS.   PETER BREIDT BREWING CO.

JACOB RUPPERT BREWERY   THE EBLING BREWING CO., INC.

JOHN F. TROMMER, INC.   GEORGE EHRET BREWERY, INC.

G. KRUEGER BREWING CO.   THE JOHN EICHLER BREWING CO.

JOSEPH HENSLER BREWING CO.   LIEBMANN BREWERIES, INC.

OLD DUTCH BREWERS, INC.

WITH THE RECENT ALLOCATION by the War Food Administration of 15% of brewers malt for beer to meet the requirements of the armed forces of the U. S., the brewers have really gone to war. Back of the allocation is a program of moderation officially sponsored by the U. S. Army and Navy and after a Coast to Coast Survey of Drinking Conditions in and around. Army Camps, published by the U. S. Office of War Information on December 30, 1942, it was reported that

> "The sale of 3.2 beer in army camps is a healthy and sensible arrangement. The fact that there is vastly less drinking among soldiers in this war than in the last war—a fact almost universally agreed to by commanders and civilian authorities alike—may stem in part from this sale of beer in camps . . . The case for 3.2 beer is presented thus by chaplains and military police alike: it provides soldiers with a mild relaxation without impairing their efficiency".

THE BREWING INDUSTRY has sponsored a nation-wide program of cooperation with the armed forces and the civilian public to encourage high standards of conduct in places where beer is sold; and has adapted the peacetime Self-Regulation program of the Brewing Industry Foundation to wartime requirements. The wartime effort is known as the Army and Navy Cooperation Program, and has reached into every state where military and naval posts or stations are located.

THE OLDEST DRUG STORE IN NEW YORK. Olliffe's, is at 6 Bowery on the west side of the Street between Pell and Doyers. Established in 1805, it occupies the same building and carries the same store fixtures. Leeches, the article for which the store has always been famous, continue to sell in quantity. The tiny squirming things bring 50c apiece. The principal buyers are customers suffering from black eyes. Every fighter in town knows of Olliffe's.

WILD ANIMALS. Louis Ruhe at 351 Bowery is the biggest dealer in wild animals in New York. He has several floors of monkeys as well as strange snakes and birds.

DIAMOND MARKET. The Diamond Market sprawls along the west side of the Bowery from Canal to Hester Streets.

Haggling, itinerant dealers swell the crowds that swarm the stores, where hundreds of jewelers and silversmiths rent space. The shouts and bids of the mob rise above the roar of the Third Avenue El.

The Bowery Diamond Market is the clearing house for mementos of dead romances. "With all my love," may run the inscription in a gold cigarette case. "My darling" will be the words etched inside a thin gold wedding band.

ALL NIGHT MISSIONS. The two best known all night Bowery Missions are Noonan's at 5 Doyers Street and the All Night Mission at 116 Bowery.

What's left of the Bowery's drifting population, those who haven't even enough money for a flop house, doze all night on the hard wooden benches in these two missions. It's a grim picture. The last time I saw it was on a snowy night last winter. Fannie Hurst and I were taken to them by Maizie Gordon, one of the Bowery's better known characters.

The night we went was cold and wet. The long narrow room where the men sat smelled of wet, steaming clothing. None of them talked, they just sat there like stone images, their faces strangely white in the half-light of dimmed electric bulbs. They looked as if they were waiting for death.

THE ONE MILE HOUSE at 1 Rivington Street gained its name a century or more ago from the fact that it stands just one mile from City Hall. But the old stone which once marked the mileage in front of the tavern has long since disappeared.

BRASS. I am afraid that the brass shops of Allen Street like the Flea Market in Paris and the famous old Caledonia in London, have a great many up-town connections. Some are merely outlet stores for big dealers. However, they are all interesting to visit, and in many you will run across fine pieces of brass and copper.

NEIGHBORHOOD HISTORY. Back in the seventeenth century, the Dutch East India Company granted all of the land on the lower east end of Manhattan Island to eight citizens from Holland. With the exception of two parcels, Corlear's Plantation and Elslandt's Farm, the grants were known as boweries.

After the stormy days of the American struggle for independence the Bowery settled back into its accustomed peaceful ways.

In 1825 the first neighborhood gangs came into existence. Dance-halls, breweries, shipyards, low dives and resorts suddenly blossomed. The Irish fire-department riots began. Dime museums appeared. Music-halls offered cheap entertainment. In 1857 the Bowery Boys and the Dead Rabbits staged their first great riot.

McGurks' famous dance-hall at Third Street and the Bowery rated a suicide a day. Billy McGlory's customers were sliding straight to hell, if one were to believe the clergymen. McGlory ran a combination saloon and dancing dive called Alhambra Hall. The Slide and the Brighton, other noted resorts, came in for their share of condemnation.

But this is all past history. Suicide Hall is now the Bowery Mission. The old-time dives have slipped into oblivion.

In their stead are to be found cheap saloons and dingy flophouses that offer a questionable roof for 10c a night.

During the day, the Bowery's drifters perch, like sleepy chickens, on curbstone and door-step. One of them, a former Virginia attorney, told me the Bowery was like the sort of woman he had always been looking for, the kind that asked no questions.

The A.W.V.S. gives the Lower East Side
current news on ration points

· THE LOWER EAST SIDE ·

THE IRISH and the Jews live side by side on the lower East Side. Al Smith grew up on Oliver Street. Around the corner was the oldest Jewish cemetery in the United States.

You can buy Irish potatoes on Oliver Street or gefülte fish on Delancey.   *   *   *

MacDOWELL'S BIRTH-PLACE. Edward MacDowell, the great American composer, was born at 220 Clinton Street. This is just on the edge of the Spanish section—a point that may explain a certain trend in his music.

ROUMANIAN CAFE. Greenberg's at 286 Broome Street, is the last of the old-time restaurants on the Lower East Side. The food, surroundings, and Mr. Greenberg himself, are happily reminiscent of gourmet nights. Among those who have enjoyed Greenberg's food in the last 50 years are Teddy Roosevelt, (when he was police commissioner), William McAdoo, Al Smith and thousands of others. A meal for two, with wine, averages $4.00.

SCARLET FEATHER PILLOWS. The rows upon rows of great square scarlet pillows that dangle from store fronts on the Lower East Side advertise bedding supplies.

Up and down the little streets around East Houston, are many dried mushroom shops, as you might expect in a locality that has a weakness for mushrooms in the cooking of gravies and soups.

Avenue A—a north and south thoroughfare that intersects East Houston — is given over to wholesale furniture houses. Farther up, just beyond Corlear's Hook Park (named after Peter Stuyvesant's bugler) you will find Goerick Street, where a few of the much-talked-of rear tenement houses still linger.

These are the slums of New York. The streets are dirty, fire-escapes cluttered with rubbish and the tenements cheerless.

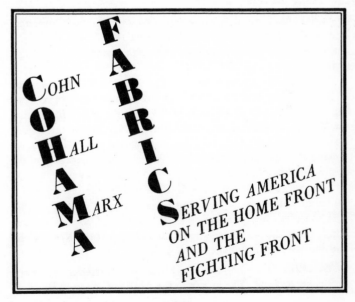

Already most of these places are becoming a thing of the past. The rehabilitation of the Lower East Side has been going on for more than ten years. The old law tenements are being replaced by clean, airy modern apartments. One of the best examples of these city housing developments is the Vladeck Houses across from the Henry Street settlement.

I hope you like to walk. The only real way to see the East Side is afoot. If you feel in the mood, turn back on Water Street and stroll down ten blocks to Oliver. In this street Al Smith played when he was a boy. Across from his house, No. 25, stands old St. James Church, where he went to Sunday Mass.

As a boy "Governor" Smith worked at the Fulton Fish Market. This market is unique. The best time to visit it is around six in the morning when the boats come in with their catch. Geographically it sprawls along Fulton Street to Peck Slip and from Front Street to the East River.

MELTING-POT. From First to Fourteenth Streets east of Third Avenue, swarms a polyglot mixture of people. Ukranians, Russians, Roumanians, Gypsies, Portuguese, Chinese, Jews and Christians mill in and out of the streets, crowd the tenements and throng the cafes.

CAFE ROYAL. Second Avenue is the Rialto of Little Roumania. It extends from Houston to 14th Street. On it are the night clubs, theaters, restaurants and stores that cater to the foreign element.

Famous among them is the Cafe Royal at 188 Second Avenue. It is one of the few restaurants in town that has been able to run a successful sidewalk cafe in the summertime. Here, after the Yiddish Theater closes, gather the intelligentsia of the Lower East Side, poets, writers, soap-box orators and actors. Long hair, flowing ties and Hamlet gestures create an atmosphere suggestive of old Greenwich Village days.

The best time to visit the Cafe Royal is Sunday night for dinner or any week-day evening toward twelve o'clock.

The serious Jewish drama is to be found at 66 Second Avenue where the audience is made up of the habitues of the Royal Cafe, and the entire performance is in Yiddish.

CEMETERIES. Two of New York's oldest cemeteries are linked to Second Avenue. The annex to the Marble Cemetery is tucked in a tiny alleyway between Second and Third Streets on the west side of the avenue.

"The street where the white peacocks walked" was the romantic title bestowed a century ago upon Second Street where the First Marble Cemetery lies. It is also the block in which Jimmy Walker trudged to school in 1897, and was awarded a sheepskin from the La Salle Academy at 44 East Second Street.

FOURTEENTH STREET is by turns the Fifth Avenue as well as the Coney Island of New York's Ghetto. Here, the playboys of Division Street go walking with their Rebeccas and Rachels. Lurid-postered moving-picture shows compete with cheap little shops.

Fifty years ago Luchow's was the smart German restaurant. The same families who came then still patronize the famous old restaurant at 110 East 14th Street.

KLEIN'S. Every woman in New York, keen on values, whether she admits it or not has bought a dress at Klein's. The store stands on the northeast corner of 14th Street and Union Square. It is an institution. There are no sales-women. Klein's caters to all classes—fat or thin, rich or poor, tall or short.

A.W.V.S. ON THE LOWER EAST SIDE. The A.W.V.S. 4th Division, Lower East Side, Roosevelt Park and Vladeck Houses Units. In this crowded and populous part of the city where children are far more common than trees and where foreign languages are more frequently heard than English, the American Women's Voluntary Services set up shop shortly after our entrance into the war.

Parent A.W.V.S. unit in the district is the Lower East Side Unit with headquarters in the Grand Street Settlement House at 283 Rivington Street, and a salvage depot just a block and a half away at 283 Stanton Street.

· OLD RUSSIA ·

THE WHITE RUSSIANS first came to Tompkins Square district in 1923. A few had been there before but the majority swarmed in after July of that year. They brought with them the customs of their country. Little restaurants which specialized in Russian food, tiny shops that sold peasant embroideries, carved wooden ornaments and Russian paper-back books. Cabarets that featured sword dances and balalaika players supplanted the conservative old New Yorkers. * * *

THE RUSSIAN KRETCHMA at 244 East 14th Street is still one of the most typically Russian cabarets. Dinner with the floor show costs $1.75 and up.

In recent years the Russian colony has become more scattered. One group is on 57th Street in the neighborhood of Carnegie Hall. Another lives around the Russian church at 121st Street and Madison Avenue, opposite Mount Morris Park. You'll find still another lot near Riverside Drive and 149th Street. In all there are about 800,000 Russians in New York City.

Here are a few restaurants and night clubs where you are likely to see them and to find good Russian food and music.

The first on my list, the Russian Tea Room at 150 West 57th Street has no music. But there are plenty of famous musicians here, for practically all of those who play at Carnegie Hall dine here. The food is very good and typically Russian. A dinner for two, with cocktails, will cost about $3.50.

The Russian Bear Restaurant at 645 Lexington Avenue is another popular dining spot for those who like Russian food and music.

A.W.V.S., PETER STUYVESANT UNIT. One of New York's most famous landmarks is the old St. Marks-on-the-Bowerie Church where Peter Stuyvesant, First Governor of New Netherlands, and other notables of the city's early history lie buried. Right across the street from the church in the heart of "Old Russia" at 166 Second Avenue, is the headquarters of one of the newest A.W.V.S. units.

· GRAMERCY PARK ·

GRAMERCY PARK has retained the spirit of old New York.

Only those with homes on the square may have the key to the park. Many of the original families use the key first presented to them. Among these are the Harpers and the Hewitts, who were born and raised in the neighborhood.

CLUB ROW. There are two famous clubs on the south side of Gramercy Park, the Players and the National Arts. If you happen to have friends who are members of either one, ask for a guest card. If you are of the masculine gender, you can visit the Players Club any day in the year, but if you are of the opposite sex, the only time you may cross the threshold is Ladies' Day, which occurs but once in twelve months.

The Players Club is the former home of Edwin Booth, the great tragedian, whose statue stands in the center of Gramercy Park. Much of the interior remains just as he left it. Utterly unchanged is his bedroom, typical of the period.

The National Arts Club is the neighborhood house of Gramercy Park. Samuel Tilden built the sober brownstone-front mansion and made it his residence until he died.

No month of the year is without an exhibition in the club galleries. Every two weeks lectures are given in the evenings; the bulletin-board will tell you the dates and subjects.

The food served in the restaurant (open if you have' a guest card) is reasonable and home-cooked.

O. HENRY'S FAVORITE EATING PLACE. The restaurant and tap-room in which O. Henry wrote a great many of his more famous short stories is Pete's Tavern at the north-east corner of Irving Place and 18th Street. The food is well-cooked and substantial. Dinner for two runs about $2.00.

TEDDY ROOSEVELT'S HOUSE at Number 28 East 20th Street is the red-brick house where Theodore Roosevelt was born.

The building has been refurnished as it was when the Roosevelt family made it their home. It is a charming place. The threshold leads you back into another century, a period in which New Yorkers knew leisurely days.

The admission is 25c. The money goes toward the upkeep of the house.

Gramercy Park was founded in 1831. It was part of a real-estate development sponsored by Samuel Ruggles. The beauty of the location and the pleasant shade of the trees attracted well-to-do families. From the time it opened, through the nineteenth century it was one of the most fashionable sections in New York. Mayor James Harper of the publishing firm lived on the west side of the park. His house is easily identified by the iron lamps in front—a distinction that marks every home of a mayor of New York.

AMERICAN SEAMAN'S FRIEND SOCIETY at 175 Fifth Avenue maintains an information service from 9 a.m. to 10 p.m. weekdays and from 2 p.m. to 10 p.m. Sundays. Call Gramercy 7-8866 for information about boarding houses, clubs, churches, hospitals, and recreational facilities. The Society prides itself on answering all questions.

A.W.V.S. GRAMERCY PARK UNIT. Straight across from the old Players Club on lovely Gramercy Park are the headquarters of the A.W.V.S. Gramercy Park Unit. The offices and workroom are located at Number 52 in two third-floor rooms of the Gramercy Park Hotel, and here thousands of garments for Army and Navy relief and other welfare agencies have been turned out during the past two years. As the women volunteers bend over long cutting tables or pedal away at their sewing machines, they can hear the melodious old chimes of the Metropolitan Towers ringing out the hours; and though they cannot hear it, they know that under the hotel in which they work there still flows the very same brook which used to water Gromessie Farm that was Gramercy Park before Samuel Ruggles had his unique inspiration way back in 1831.

This row of trees cutting through Madison Square Park
follows the line of the old Boston Post Road.

· MADISON SQUARE ·

I HAVE OFTEN THOUGHT that I would like to live on Madison Square. There is a great deal of charm to the little park in which O. Henry spent so much of his time and found so much to write about. There are tall trees, fresh and green in the spring, a tiny bit of grass and flowers at certain seasons of the year, and rows of park benches crowded with odd characters.

Some amusing little shops linger in the neighborhood and still left are several interesting restaurants.

For local color on the square there is the fine old Jerome mansion, now the Manhattan Club at Madison Avenue and 26th Street, where Winston Churchill's mother, Lady Randolph Churchill lived as Miss Jennie Jerome. Close by is the Metropolitan Life Building. To the south is the Flatiron Building at 23rd Street and Broadway, once the sensation of New York.

BAZAR FRANCAIS. This is a French hardware shop established in 1877. If you like casseroles, you will find every type stocked in this little shop at 666 Sixth Avenue. It deals in real French baking-dishes of all sizes. It also handles some very nice pot-au-feu chafing-dishes of copper. They are good for Welsh rabbits as well as petite marmite, the dish for which they were originally made.

SKIN SOAP AND CREAM. A famous formula, concocted by a great skin specialist of thirty years ago, is used in the making of shampoos and creams at Bagoe's Drug Store, 86 Madison Avenue.

George Bagoe, the present proprietor, was born in the little frame house which sheltered the original drug store at 29th Street and Fourth Avenue. His father was the recognized pharmacist of the Victorian era.

Mr. Bagoe is a very pleasant man whose avocation in life is collecting old photographs. He owns one of the largest and finest groups of early American photographs in the United States. The collection is kept in a safe in his store. If you like unusual pictures, ask Mr. Bagoe to show you some of his.

BELLEVUE INN. This tiny sandwich shop at 445 First Avenue is supported by the internes and nurses at Bellevue, just across the street. The place is the usual soda-counter, lunch-room type, but I like to visit it, to pick up hospital gossip and to watch the people.

The Madison Square section and the East Twenties are rich in contrasting material. For high lights we have Bellevue Hospital, the Municipal Lodging House at 432 East 25th Street, the old stronghold of the Gas House Gang around 21st Street and First Avenue, and the morgue on 26th Street and First Avenue.

BABA NESHANS. Following an almost universal custom of centralizing nationalities in a definite location, nearly all the Armenians, Turks and Persians are in one of two places: first, the section of Washington Street which starts at the Battery and runs to 14th Street; and second, the district lying between 26th and 34th Streets, bounded on the west by Sixth Avenue and east by Fourth Avenue. It is to the latter we are going for lunch.

Practically every other house is a restaurant. Our favorite

Armenian place is Baba Neshans at 48 East 29th Street. The walls are hung with rich-hued Turkish and Armenian embroideries, and about the small tables are seated numerous sleek Persian and Turkish gentlemen, who flirt with plump creamy-skinned ladies, boasting too abundant curves and long black Oriental eyes. Try the Shish Kebab. It is 90c a portion.

TAP-ROOM. Those who do not care for Turkish food will like the Tap-Room in the back of the Prince George Hotel at 14 East 28th Street. The orders are generous, fresh and moderately priced.

PEASANT VILLAGE. Next door to the Prince George is the side-entrance to a matter-of-fact office building in which lies one of the most fascinating out-of-the-way stores. The official address is 245 Fifth Avenue and the name Mitteldorfer Straus' Peasant Village.

Mr. Straus is a native of Richmond. He went to Paris to study art, spending his summers sketching in little peasant villages. Each trip home found him laden with inexpensive gifts. People were caught by the novelties. He decided to make a business of importing peasant products.

GUNN AND LATCHFORD'S at 323 Fifth Avenue is a tantalizing spot. They carry an amazing stock of fabrics that include rare brocades patterned in silver and gold, hand-work crewel embroideries, tapestries and hand-woven linen by the yard.

BUTTERFLIES. The little shop at 256 Fifth Avenue handles butterflies of every description at all prices.

FLOWERS BY THE WHOLESALE. Through these blocks from Broadway west of Sixth Avenue in the Twenties are to be found the wholesale flower-shops of town. Little and big stores that deal in golden yellow daffodils by the carload, hold bargain sales in calla-lilies, and move American Beauty roses by the truckful. There is no need to list the shops separately. They are too numerous.   *   *   *

EVERY old newspaperman in town remembers the West Twenties for one reason: Mouquin's Restaurant. It stood, until prohibition closed it, on the southeast corner of 28th Street and Sixth Avenue. The finest wines and liqueurs in the world were listed, and among the chief patrons were James Gibbons Hunecker, the famous music critic, Anna Held, George M. Cohan, Freddie Gebhardt and his lady-love, Lily Langtry, Diamond Jim Brady, Stanford White and the Davis brothers, Richard Harding and Charles Belmont, who had an apartment on West 30th Street. Another patron was O. Henry, living at that time in the Caledonia Apartments at 28 West 26th Street. Stanford White's studio was in the tower of Madison Square Garden, which then stood at 26th Street and Fourth Avenue.

In years gone by these streets, from 23rd to about 34th, west of Broadway, were peopled with fashionable New Yorkers. The brownstone houses now occupied by Syrian restaurants were once the homes of the Four Hundred, in the days when it really was the Four Hundred.

· *MURRAY HILL* ·

FOR MANY YEARS Murray Hill and the name of Morgan were synonymous. The elder J. P. Morgan lived in the big brownstone front at Madison and 37th Street. One of the few detached houses left in New York, it has stood, blinds drawn, garden deserted, ever since Mr. Morgan's death. Adjoining it, on the 36th Street side of the block, is the handsome white stone building of the famous Morgan Library now owned by the city. Most of its treasures have been taken out of town in anticipation of possible air raids but you will still find very interesting collections on view. The big Florentine room which used to be Mr. Morgan's private library is well worth seeing. Admission is free. The hours are from 9 to 5 week-days. It is closed the month of August.

The section known as Murray Hill extends from 34th Street to 42nd Street. Its boundary lines are Fifth and Third Avenues. While we are in this neighborhood I'm going to take you out of bounds for a few moments to 34th Street and Broadway. This was once the heart of the theatrical district. It is now a very busy shopping center. Hundreds of thousands swarm through it daily. On the northwest corner of 34th Street and Broadway is Macy's, the biggest department store in the world. This store is a New York institution. One of its boasts is that you can buy anything you want here, from a house to a live chicken.

Ride the escalator to the second floor and watch the crowds as you go up. Then you will understand why Macy's does millions of dollars worth of business each year.

Across from Macy's on the southwest corner of Broadway and 34th Street is Saks 34th Street and beyond that Gimbel Bros. the first department store in the world to sell fine art. Gimbel's had the disposal of the entire Hearst collection. Their art galleries on the fifth floor are like a museum. The store also holds exhibitions and sales in the old Jay Gould mansion at 579 Fifth Avenue.

The Gould home, a perfect example of Victorian luxury, is well worth a visit.

There are still many brownstones of the Gould period on the quiet side streets of Murray Hill. Some of them, like the former George Baker home, are occupied by organizations and clubs. The late Mr. Baker's house is now the headquarters of the Henry Street Visiting Nurse Service.

Organizations on Murray Hill for the men and women in service include the following:

*   *   *

SOLDIERS AND SAILORS CLUB at 283 Lexington Avenue (between 36th and 37th Streets) supplies double and triple rooms for servicemen at 50c per person a night. The restaurant canteen (open from 7 a.m. to 8 p.m.) serves a complete breakfast for 20c and a three-course luncheon or dinner (soup, meat, salad, dessert, beverage) for 40c or 45c. You can get eggs and bacon at any time for 20c, sandwiches for 5c and up.

MERCHANT MARINE RECREATION CENTER is at the Andrew Furuseth Club, 30 East 37th Street. This four-story building is open to merchant seamen from 9 a.m. to 12 p.m. daily. You pay 50c for a tasty and substantial luncheon or dinner served by the A.W.V.S. This includes soup, meat, vegetables, salad, dessert, and coffee. A la carte sandwiches are 10c and 15c. You can buy beer (10c for a large glass) and soft drinks at the bar. There's no charge for the entertainment—billiards, games and dancing (with attractive hostesses).

The Recreation Center is sponsored by the United Seaman's Service of 39 Broadway. Apply at the center for admittance to the two rest homes for seamen veterans of enemy action and convalescents discharged from marine hospitals. There's no charge at either of these homes—one on the Kermit Roosevelt estate in Oyster Bay, the other on the C. Suydam Cutting estate in Gladstone, New Jersey.

NEW YORK CITY DEFENSE RECREATION COMMITTEE, 99 Park Avenue at 40th Street, is open from 9 to 9 every day. On Saturday nights the telephone service (Mu 3-6900) remains open from 9 p.m. to 2 a.m. to supply men with information about rooms only. Go to 99 Park for free tickets to theaters, movies, sporting events, broadcasts, sightseeing trips, dances and concerts. A complete information service tells you about sleeping accommodations and how to get free personal instruction on any high school or college subject or hobby, if you'd like to advance your rank in the service.

OFFICERS' CLUB OF THE ARMY AND NAVY, 23 Park Avenue. Officers can receive courtesy cards to this club by applying to the Officers Service Committee at the Hotel Commodore. This card entitles you to use the club in the five-story brownstone building which also houses the Advertising Club. The hours are weekdays from 9 a.m. to 11 p.m. During June, July and August the club is closed on Saturdays as well as Sundays.

INFORMATION PLEASE. No matter what your question or who you are, the ladies at the A.W.V.S. Information Center will give you the answer if they can. Just call Murray Hill 3-9800 (the A.W.V.S. national headquarters at 345 Madison Avenue) and ask for the Information Center. The thousands of questions put to them range from queries about shipping packages to the armed forces to naming a minister to tie the wedding knot.

THE "AGE OF INNOCENCE" HOTEL. Edith Wharton would have been in her element if she had stopped at the Murray Hill Hotel on Park Avenue and 40th Street. Mid-Victorian ladies live here. Lunch or Sunday morning breakfast in the big dining room on the 40th Street side, is an experience. The atmosphere heavily gracious.

If you have a feeling, as I have, for picturesque houses with interesting histories you will enjoy walking by Mrs. Cholmeley-Jones' delightful old home at 152 East 38th Street. It was built in 1845. President James Monroe once spent his summers here. Both it and the adjoining house, Number 150, have been turned into pure Regency by Russell Pettengill. They share the same garden. Cass Canfield, president of Harper Bros. has Mrs. Cholmeley-Jones' home under lease. Major George Fielding Eliot, the news commentator, lives in Number 150.

MURRAY HILL COVENANT. Famous in the history of this neighborhood has been the Murray Hill Covenant, drawn up by a group of residents in 1847. In it they agreed to keep the district purely residential and to prevent anything taller than a two-story building from being erected in the locality. That has long since been broken.

Murray Hill is full of delightful, unexpected courtyards and interesting homes. Malvina Hoffman's studio at the end of

Sniffen Court, off East 36th Street, makes you think of Paris.

The tip end of Murray Hill is flanked by the only street in the world that has four sidewalks—East 42nd Street between 1st and 2nd Avenues. In this neighborhood is that amazing group of apartment units called Tudor City. Their very size is bewildering.

It is a locality of contrasts. To the south of Tudor City is the famous Corcoran Roost district on 39th Street just off 2nd Avenue. On 42nd Street and 1st Avenue once stood the notorious House of Blazes, haunt of gangs.

To the north are the slaughter-houses. They extend from 47th to 49th on 1st Avenue. Glancing in the direction of the East River, one may see the jagged lines of the Hog Bank Rocks, the beginning of Welfare Island, home of the city alms-house and hospitals. Welfare or Blackwell's Island, as it was formerly called, extends from 49th to 70th Streets. The 49th Street end of 1st Avenue, known as Beekman Hill, is now one of the fashionable residential sections of town.

JOE AND ROSA'S ITALIAN-FRENCH RESTAURANT. This couple once had a delicatessen with a table in the rear for customers who wanted to take their soup in the store. Now it's all restaurant. The food is still delicious and the restaurant popular with the newspaper crowd from the Daily News and the Mirror. The address is 745 3rd Avenue.

THE EMPIRE STATE BUILDING is an outpost of Murray Hill. It stands on the southwest corner of the neighborhood of 34th Street and 5th Avenue. I don't need to tell you which corner. You can't miss its shining chromium and black shaft. Its tower affords the best view of New York in the city. Admission is $1.10 but service men are admitted free Wednesdays and Sundays, half price other days. It is the tallest building in the world, soaring 1,250 feet into the air. It is also famous for being Al Smith's business headquarters.

WEDDING GIFTS. For years and years Ovington's, at 39th Street and Fifth Avenue, has been the store New Yorkers went to when they wanted to find wedding presents of quality. Its name is synonymous with fine china and glassware, unusual little occasional tables and rare lamps.

A.W.V.S. MIDTOWN BUSINESS GIRLS UNIT. Just on the edge of Murray·Hill is one of the youngest and most ambitious

A.W.V.S. units. Known as the Midtown Business Girls Unit because its members are all employed in offices in the midtown section of Manhattan, this unit makes its headquarters on the second floor of a "taxpayer" at 201 East 42nd Street, and its offices, including the workshop, are open Monday through Friday from 12 noon to 2 p.m. and from 5:30 to 8 p.m.

Servicemen will find attractive lounges in the Pennsylvania and Grand Central Stations where they may eat, read, write, play cards, or just talk between trains. Sponsored by U.S.O.

THE SIGHT-SEEING CANTEEN meets every Sunday afternoon (usually at 1:30 p.m.) at Sloane House Y.M.C.A., 34th Street at 9th Avenue. Servicemen are taken on free sight-seeing tours of the city (either on bicycles or with couriers via the subway.) The groups return to Sloane House at 5 p.m. for refreshments and entertainment. There is no charge. You'll also enjoy the Sunday afternoon co-ed picnics arranged by the Canteen.

· *MY OWN NEIGHBORHOOD* ·

I HAPPEN TO LIVE on 57th Street and Park Avenue but when I speak of my neighborhood I think of the section which extends from 42nd to 61st Streets east of Broadway. For this is the part of town where I do most of my roaming after office hours.

A favorite haunt of mine is 1129 Sixth Avenue between 43rd and 44th Streets. It is a glorified notion store and the huge sign SOUVENIRS on the window will help you locate it. Here you will find bargains in anything from razor blades or shoe polish to needles, thread and soaps.

This section of 6th Avenue, as you will notice, also abounds in back-number magazine stores, employment agencies and shooting galleries.

The Ritz Grill in the basement of the Ritz-Carlton Hotel at 46th Street and Madison Avenue, is another favorite of mine. It is handy for quick lunches. For some reason, probably for the very good one that the Ritz Grill happens to be in their neighborhood, you'll find flocks of magazine editors, publishers, authors' agents and authors lunching here.

A.W.V.S. WAR SHOP. If you like unusual accessories try the A.W.V.S. War Shop at 14 East 52nd Street across from Henri's restaurant. Unique change purses, for instance. The A.W.V.S. has them for its members and the public. They are made of scarlet and blue grosgrain ribbon mounted on a frame and are cut in a trick way to carry both bills and change in separate compartments. Price $1.25.

This shop also has some very smart natural cravenette cloth raincoats. The A.W.V.S. girls wear them. The public also may. Price $10.00.

HENRI'S. If you happen to land there around noon, lunch at Henri's just opposite. The cooking, as you may have guessed from the name, is French and very delicious. Henri is about in the class with the old Maillard's, now out of existence.

KITCHEN GADGETS. If you like household novelties you will revel in Hammacher and Schlemmer's store at 145 East 57th Street. It's a perfect hardware store in which to shop for thank-

you gifts, things like little individual earthenware coffee pots which make coffee taste the way it smells.

THE RIGHT FURNITURE. W. & J. Sloane, at 5th Avenue and 47th Street, is one of New York's oldest and finest furniture stores. To say that your home was furnished by Sloane is to say you have bought the best in taste and quality that money could buy. Whether or not you are buying furniture a visit to this store is educational. Many people go to Sloane's, as they would to the Metropolitan Museum of Art, to see beautiful things.

ANTIQUE JEWELRY. If you like antique designs in jewelry you will appreciate the Harris jewelry shop at 25 East 48th Street. Charles Harris, the proprietor, has a fascinating collection of ancient poison rings. They are not for sale. He also has (for sale) beautiful copies of fine antique necklaces, ear-rings and bracelets. His specialty is a modern version of antique wedding rings; two little gold hands clasped over a heart, three rings in one (faith, hope and charity), and a replica of the Victorian chaperon ring.

Incidentally, Mr. Harris is one of the few jewelers in this country who can successfully repair enamelled jewelry.

ANTIQUES. Along 3rd Avenue from 50th to 61st Streets, you will find antique row. Any and every kind of an antique in the world seems to have gravitated to the hundreds of second hand stores which line both sides of the avenue.

Just this side of 3rd Avenue at 151 East 50th Street, is the famous Versailles Night Club.

There's a charming little court on the southwest corner of 51st Street and 3rd Avenue filled with antique shops. Richard Croker, the Tammany leader built this corner more than fifty years ago.

Kitty-cornered across the street from the court is the 51st Street police station through which sift the various crimes of the fashionable East Side.

At 54th Street between 3rd and Lexington Avenues, is El Morocco mentioned in another chapter. A block further north on East 55th Street, just beyond Victor Miller's Louis Quatorze antique shop at 155 East 55th Street, is The Blue Angel, a new night-club run by a Frenchman who knows his omelets. He had the wit to employ Mme. Romaine. She is there every night from ten on concocting delicious French rum omelets. During the day she manages Maison Louis de Lyon, her own little French tea shop at 137½ East 56th Street near Lexington Avenue. Her specialty is real French Brioche which she bakes herself.

Across the street from Mme. Romaine is the Chateaubriand, a delightful French restaurant at 148 E. 56th Street. A great many Continental people like Somerset Maugham, Mme. Manuelo Alonzo, wife of the Basque tennis player, and Edward Wasserman eat here.

Two interesting foreign restaurants where I often lunch are the Three Crowns at 12 East 54th Street (famous for its smorgasbord) and the Restaurant Suisse at 22 East 54th Street, a quaint little place where the husband, Celestin Servant, is the chef.

If you want to spend money and feel in the mood for an elaborate meal I suggest any one of the following restaurants, each a gourmet haunt:

The Marguery at 270 Park Avenue.

Voissin at 375 Park Avenue.

La Belle Meuniere at 12 East 52nd Street.

Passy at 28 East 63rd Street.

Opposite the St. Regis is a charming little French restaurant known as Le Pavillon at 5 East 55th Street, which I also recommend.

CARTIER. On the southeast corner of 5th Avenue and 52nd Street stands the most famous French jewelry firm in the world, Cartier, jewelers to the courts of Europe and Asia. The bronze clock, ornamented by the coq of France and the American eagle, which juts out from the second story level is symbolic of the friendship which has existed between America and France.

A little over a quarter of a century ago a great mansion looking like some ancient palace transported from Italy stood on this corner.

Quite fittingly, what was once the mansion of a millionaire became the American headquarters for this famous French jewelry firm. Attractive, and not too expensive jewelry novelties are displayed in the counter show cases. The rare pieces are in slim wall cases, fantastically beautiful things like the "Nuptial Imperial Crown of Russia" worn by Catherine the Great on her wedding day; the Blue Venus, a 17th Century Spanish gem carved out of one single block of sapphire and the Ruby Buddha, carved during the 15th Century for the Emperor of China.

Cartier has had and still has illustrious patrons. King Edward VII. was responsible for the opening of its London house. J. P.

Cartier

$\mathcal{E}$ngagement ring, insignia, service watch — or fashionable jewel — you'll find a superb selection at Cartier, and at the price you want to pay. . . . Illustrated: The first ladies' self-winding waterproof wrist watch — shock-resistant, dust-proof, non-magnetic — a 17 jewel little beauty in stainless steel, $65; a gold patriotic insignia, $42; and one of a large selection of diamond engagement rings, gem stones, from $87.

Fifth Avenue and Fifty-Second Street, New York 22.

Morgan, the elder, saw that it established an American branch.

In four years Cartier will celebrate its century, and what is, rather unique, especially in New York, is the fact that the ownership has not changed in that time. It has always remained in the Cartier family.

COTY. For civilians visiting New York, Coty offers a thrill in its 5th Avenue Salon at 612 5th Avenue (in Rockefeller Center). Here is a perfume-testing bar where you may sniff the famous Coty fragrances and try them on yourself. Treatment rooms for facials have wonderful squashy chaise lounges and Muzak to further relax you while you are ministered to by skin and make-up experts. The famous Coty "Refresher Service" is given here. For $1.50 you can have a quick pick-up facial while a maid presses and freshens up your dress and a valet shines your shoes. You are given a complimentary makeup and touch of your favorite Coty perfume and may re-do your hair.

The fabulous Women's Military Services Club for WACS, WAVES, SPARS, Women Marines, Army and Navy Nurses and women in other uniforms of the United Nations is housed in the historic old Whitelaw Reid mansion at 50th Street and Madison Avenue.

They say Coty spent $100,000 in making possible this "home away from home" for service girls. Beds at 50c a night for enlisted women are available and three meals a day at below-cost prices are served to both enlisted women and officers in the beautiful old dining room with its Augustus St. Gauden's sculptures, and paintings by Edwin Abbey. Weekly tea dances are held in the ballroom.

Discover
with delight . . .

. . . the serene, "other-world" aura
of Coty Fifth Avenue.

. . . the bliss of "just looking" when
you prefer . . . the expert advice
when you wish it.

. . . the vast scope—even today—
of Coty creations: exquisite perfumes, flattering make-up, unusual
gifts . . . all styled with Coty chic.

COTY FIFTH-AVENUE

ROCKEFELLER CENTER, FIFTH AVE. AT 49TH ST.

the loveliest shop on the Avenue

The building itself is a landmark for, besides being the White-law Reid mansion, it is one of four attached houses that formed the first co-operative apartment house in New York. You can't miss it, a big brownstone Florentine palace rimming three sides of a court opposite the Madison Avenue end of St. Patrick's Cathedral.

ELIZABETH ARDEN. 5th Avenue in the blocks between 54th and 56th Streets might almost be called Beauty Row. Three of the country's most famous makers of beauty products and advocates of beauty schools: Elizabeth Arden, Richard Hudnut and Helena Rubinstein have their establishments in this section.

In addition to her famous beauty school Miss Arden is now featuring a special "Furlough morning."

You arrive at the Salon on the dot of 9:30 in the morning a little tired and panicky. You are taken in hand by a pleasant, white-gowned attendant and for the entire morning you are treated and fussed over by experts whose competent hands keep doing things to make you feel more wonderful every minute.

You begin with a massage. The aches and kinks and taut nerves seem to melt away under the firm, but gentle touch of those strong and skillful hands. You don't remember whether you actually fell asleep or not, but you are awakened from your blissful lethargy with the Scotch Hose. You're not sleepy any longer. This revitalizing treatment really wakes you up.

Now to the Hair Shop. You are brushed and rubbed and scrubbed and shampooed until your hair fairly squeaks with cleanliness. Next for the setting in the lovely new hair style which you have selected in the hair book. You know exactly what it will look like, for the pictures and sketches of each coiffure show front, back, side and detailed views. As you sit under the drier, your nails are given attention.

With the pins still in your hair you are taken to a private little room where nimble fingers work on your face. Tiny lines disappear as if by magic. The Egg Mask treatment makes your

IT'S HAPPENING TO *You*

You change imperceptibly in spite of yourself, but only you can determine whether the change is for the better ... An Efficiency Plan will chart a health and beauty program to make a brighter future more secure ... Since time is vital, this plan is concentrated, gets down to essentials fast. Here minutes are magic and every minute is well spent.

Plan A ... 8 class lessons, plus private "Special Emphasis" treatments, coordinate health and beauty building in a highly individualized program. You receive an Efficiency Kit containing the Essentials for home care of the skin ...50.00

Plan B ...a program of scientific relaxation plus time-saving personal grooming for health and beauty ... a face treatment, body massage, shampoo, wave, and manicure every week for 4 weeks ... 32.50

Plan C ...concise class instruction in new, swift methods of developing health, beauty, and good grooming: including an Efficiency Kit containing the Essentials for home care of the skin. Eight lessons ... 25.00

Enroll today at the Elizabeth Arden Salon

TO SERVE YOU WELL WHILE YOU SERVE OTHERS

An Efficiency Kit containing the essential preparations for skin care ...FOR DRY SKIN – Ardena Cleansing Cream, Ardena Skin Lotion, Ardena Orange Skin Cream, Ardena Astringent Oil, and Ardena Feather-Light Foundation, 5.50. Kits also for OILY, NORMAL and BLEMISHED SKIN from 5.50 to 6.00 (All prices plus taxes)

Elizabeth Arden

skin glow with new radiance. Finally, your make-up. It blends perfectly with the color of your dress. Your reflection in the mirror leaves you breathless.

Then on with your dress. The pins are taken out. Your hair is brushed and combed and brushed until each strand lies obediently in place. Now your hat—at just the proper angle. As you write out your check for $10.00 (the cost of the entire morning) you are sprayed with your favorite perfume.

THE HUDNUT SCHOOL, at 693 5th Avenue is next door to Elizabeth Arden's. Ann Delafield, the head of it, has focused on business women. I personally witnessed some of the transformations in a six-weeks' night success course I took at this school. I saw fat girls made thin and thin ones made pleasantly round. Of course it wasn't all Miss Delafield. Will power and steady exercising helped. But none of it could have been accomplished without Ann Delafield's sane planning.

The intensive day course which lasts six weeks is $200.00. You go to school every day from Monday to Friday. However, if you can spare only one night a week, there is a course for you, too. A two-hour session, one night a week for six weeks costs $40.00.

HELENA RUBINSTEIN. A few doors north of Hudnut's is the Helena Rubinstein salon at 715 Fifth Avenue.

Under the direction of Miss Mala Rubinstein, niece of Madame Rubinstein, you will find here facilities for the beauty and health of every part of the body. Many of the services offered at this salon are individually planned for the needs of each woman. Custom-made facial treatments range from a short (three-quarter hour) pick up treatment at $3.50 to a longer corrective treatment at $6.00.

The Sun treatment is another service available at the Rubinstein Salon. You lie in an individual bed of snow-white sand, and let the ultra-violet rays stream down their health and energy upon you. This service is $3.50.

The Hair Styling Salon on the 6th floor is under the direction of Monsieur Michel, a hair stylist who is both artistic and original.

You can also have a manicure, or pedicure, a foot treatment

and chiropody. The foot treatment is immensely restful, comprising a deep, soothing massage and a foot masque, which is invigorating and cooling to tired feet.

THE MUSEUM OF MODERN ART at 11 West 53rd Street is famous for its exhibitions of contemporary art. Besides a permanent collection of works of Cezanne, Van Gogh, Picasso and contemporary American artists, the museum stages all sorts of special exhibits, many of them industrial.

It runs straight through the block on the ground where stood, up to a few years ago, the home of John D. Rockefeller. There is a pleasant garden back of the museum where you may have luncheon or tea on warm days.

OGILVIE SISTERS. Familiar New York City landmark at 604 Fifth Avenue is the well-known curved glass window of Ogilvie Sisters' Salon.

Outstanding in the field of hair culture and care, the famous sisters have built their pioneering line of hair and scalp preparations into a successful business.

That these specialists, the Ogilvie sisters, are not a myth is easy

to prove. Clients and visitors are always delighted when they meet the different sisters at the Salon. An Ogilvie Method "exclusively-for-men's" Shop *does* exist at 50 East 42nd Street.

THE CHICKEN KOOP RESTAURANT, at 37 West 58th Street, between 5th and 6th Avenues, is the original restaurant where chicken was fried to order and could be eaten with the fingers.

For thirteen years it has drawn its patrons from every part of the United States. All who like to eat chicken with their fingers, flock to this gay and cheerful eating place.

Mrs. Belle Feinberg, the owner and manager, has her produce daily from her own farm in New Jersey.

THE SAVOY-PLAZA HOTEL at 59th Street and 5th Avenue.

The Cafe Lounge lists among its regular entertainers Dwight Fiske and Morton Downey. This year, however, the Savoy-Plaza is paying homage to South America by having Clemente's Marimba Band for dancing, while Narita, exotic Puerto Rican adds color via her songs. From 5:00 p.m. to closing hour one may dance to Joseph C. Smith's orchestra and the Marimba band.

THE LONGCHAMPS RESTAURANTS, scattered about New York, have always maintained a high standard of food and service. They are patronized by an interesting type of clientele, according to the locality in which they are placed.

The one at 59th Street and Madison Avenue in my own neighborhood, is where I go often for dinner. I especially recommend their calf's liver simmered in butter, with French fried potatoes.

RUMPELMAYERS, 50 Central Park South. To go for Sunday morning breakfast, is to start the day with as intriguing a bit of atmosphere as may be found in this city. A part of the St. Moritz Hotel on West 59th Street corner of 6th Avenue, it is distinctly foreign and is at once gay, social and intimate. By eleven o'clock the place is jammed with varying nationalities. All languages float about one. There is a marked sprinkling of Army and Navy Officers, and the food is delicious. The Continental breakfast— fruit, brioche or sweet rolls, jams and coffee—is my favorite. Do not miss the experience.

LA SALLE DU BOIS. One of the best upper-medium priced restaurants in my neighborhood is La Salle du Bois at 36 East 60th Street. Dinner runs around $2.00 but it is worth double the price. The cooking is French and excellent. The atmosphere is on the swank side.

PATRICIA MURPHY'S. A lot for a little money should be the motto of Miss Murphy's restaurant at 33 E. 60th Street. Dinner ranges from $1.00 to $1.50. This means from soup to nuts. The cooking is delicious. Filipino boys give quick service. The only complaint I have to make about this restaurant is its popularity. Unless you get there early you have to wait in line.

ART GALLERIES. 57th Street between 5th and Lexington Avenues is known as picture gallery row. You will find most of the leading art galleries of the town in this section.

59th Street between these same two avenues is known as book-shop row. There are pleasant little book-stalls to browse over and old prints, like those on the Paris quays, to enjoy.

My favorite 59th Street book dealer is A. Langer of the Franklin Book Shop.

CENTRAL PARK. The 768 acres of land stretching their green length in the heart of the largest city in the United States have been but little touched since they were first portioned off as a central park in 1862. The boundary-lines are 59th Street, Central Park West, 110th Street and 5th Avenue.

The same delightful early Victorian amusements and background prevail in Central Park today. You will find the lake dotted by rowboats in the summer and crowded with skaters when frozen over.

There are three good-sized bodies of water in Central Park: the main lake which extends almost across the park from 77th Street on the west side to 72nd; on the east, the pond near 59th Street where ice-skating also prevails in the winter; and Harlem

Lake at the extreme north end of the park, up near 110th Street.

The main entrance is at 65th Street and 5th Avenue.

That prim old brown-brick building which faces you as you turn toward the Zoo is the Arsenal. It was used during the Civil War as headquarters for troops being rushed south. The state armory occupied it for many years. It is now owned and tenanted by the department of parks and Dr. Harry Nimphius, the Zoo keeper.

I like the cafeteria incorporated in the Zoo center. It is pleasant to eat here Sunday mornings in the summer. There is a terrace and small tables shaded by bright colored umbrellas.

From the latter part of June through summer, concerts are given free in the Mall by the Goldman band. They are held three times a week and begin promptly at eight o'clock. Park benches are lined up in front of the concert stand but there are never enough seats even though thousands of benches are supplied. If you want to be comfortable get there early. The music is excellent and the crowd interesting—babies, children, sweethearts, husbands, wives, and old and young. The attendance averages 25,000.

One of the largest of the sixteen baseball diamonds is at this end of the park, below the Sheepfold. Soccer is also played here as well as football, depending on the season. The contestants are usually members of opposing high-school teams. There are also 34 tennis courts on which to play. For rules, inquire at Room 201 in the Arsenal Building on 5th Avenue and East 64th Street.

On 5th Avenue and 91st Street, facing Central Park, is New York's most outstanding private residence, the Andrew Carnegie home. It is the only house left on 5th Avenue with a private garden.

THE METROPOLITAN MUSEUM OF ART takes up more than one-third of a million square feet on the east side of the park at 81st Street and 5th Avenue. It is open from 10 to 5 week-days. Saturdays until 6. Sundays 1 to 6. Admission is free.

If you wish to get lunch, there is a cafeteria in the basement. I won't tell you what is in the museum, since you probably know already and if you do not, a guide-book purchased at the door will give you the story.

CANTEENS AND SERVICE CLUBS are scattered through my neighborhood as you will see from the following listing:

WAVES prettying themselves at Elizabeth Arden's make-up bar in the Service Women's Canteen at the Biltmore

SERVICE WOMEN'S CENTER. The mezzanine at the Biltmore has become the Service Women's Center for both officers and enlisted women in every branch of the Services of the United Nations. It is sponsored and staffed by members of the Metropolitan Association of Kappa Kappa Gamma, who keep it open from noon till 9:00, dealing out information of where to go to get theatre tickets, invitations to dances, where to go to cash a check and shop. It's a homey place full of comfortable couches, writing tables, telephones, and best of all, a refuge to repair the ravages of a day of sightseeing.

And that is where Elizabeth Arden comes to the rescue. The lounge which she has donated to the Service Women's Center has pink walls and cocoa carpet and pink and green plaid slip covers. It was decorated by Virginia Connor. It's a room that makes you feel good. It lifts your spirits and the girls like it. Along one wall is a mirrored make-up bar with a row of little chartreuse-topped stools and on the bar a constant, never failing supply of every Elizabeth Arden aid to loveliness — creams, lotions, lipsticks, powder, and all the rest. The make-up bar, in fact, is a very active spot.

THE SHIPS' SERVICE COMMITTEE at 22 East 47th Street serves as a liaison between men of the Allied fleet and the facilities of New York. They function under the Morale Office of the Navy and offer planned entertainment including dances at the large hotels for entire crews of Allied ships. Requests for these parties should be made through a ship's officer at the downtown office of the committee, 90 Church Street.

THE OFFICERS' SERVICE COMMITTEE is located at the Commodore Hotel, Lexington Avenue and 42nd Street. Here officers may obtain half price tickets for the theater and reduced rate tickets for opera, sports and concerts. By presenting these at the box office, the officer can buy admission tickets at substantial reductions for himself and his date. The Committee also provides courtesy cards to city and country clubs, arranges hotel and resort accommodations, and provides general information about New York. The Dance Committee entertains at a formal dance at a leading hotel every Saturday night from 9 to 1. You can bring your date, or dance with the hostesses. There is no charge. An officers' cabaret is held every Saturday night at the Commodore from 9:30 to 1:00 with dancing and entertainment. You pay $1.10 each for yourself and your date. Drinks are extra.

THE DUG-OUT CLUB at 235 East 52nd Street welcomes servicemen in all the Allied forces from 8 a.m. to 11 p.m. every day including Sunday. The club was opened in 1920 to help rehabilitate men disabled in the last war. Now men in the service can obtain single rooms at 75c a night, double rooms at 50c. Home-cooked dinners are served from 5:30 to 8:30 p.m. at a nominal charge. You can get a tasty meal for 40c. Telephone ELdorado 5-9831 for room reservations.

HOSPITALITY CENTER. All uniformed women of the Allied Nations are invited to the Hospitality Center for service-women at the Y.W.C.A., Lexington Avenue at 53rd Street. This special lounge on the ground floor is open all the time. In addition service-women are allowed to use the Y.W.C.A. facilities (such as swimming-pool, parties, educational classes, and dances) without charge.

A.W.V.S. I don't have to walk outside of my own hotel, the Ritz Tower, to run into the American Women's Voluntary Services, since the hotel itself provides space for a number of the organization's free training courses, including Code, Standard Red Cross First Aid, and Nutrition.

About the same distance from my hotel, walking west, is Reuben's Restaurant at 6 East 58th Street, which also contributes basement space to the A.W.V.S. for classes in War Service Photography.

A.W.V.S. GREATER N. Y. HEADQUARTERS. Across the street on the second floor of the annex to the Savoy-Plaza Hotel, are the A.W.V.S. Greater New York Headquarters, 11 East 58th Street. Here are the administrative offices of the Greater New York organization presided over by Mrs. Edgar Leonard, Chairman, and Mrs. Alfred F. Hess, co-chairman.

A.W.V.S. MANHATTAN HEADQUARTERS, 39 West 57th Street. After you've left 11 East 58th Street, why not walk a bit further for a look at the borough headquarters. You will find the map in the window particularly interesting for it shows you,

better than any words, how this service organization truly blankets our city from corner to corner.

OPEN HOUSE FOR OFFICERS at the Hotel Delmonico, 502 Park Avenue, every day from 12 noon to midnight. Dances are held Tuesday and Thursday nights at 8:00 p.m. in the club room. Friday nights a formal dance is held in the ballroom of the hotel. You may attend free dancing classes Monday night at 8:00 p.m. Saturday and Sunday afternoons at 4:00 p.m. there are cocktail parties.

THE OFFICERS' CLUB OF NEW YORK is open from 11:00 a.m. to 2:00 a.m. every day at the Sherry-Netherland Hotel, 5th Avenue and 59th Street. All commissioned officers of the United Nations are welcome. The club rooms are on the floor below the main floor of the hotel. They include a lounge, writing room, reading room, bridge and game rooms. Showers and dressing rooms are free of charge.

FOR MERCHANT SEAMEN. Merchant seamen of the United Nations are invited to the Tuesday night canteen at the Ritz

Tower, Park Avenue and 57th Street. As its name implies the canteen is open Tuesday nights from 8:00 p.m. until midnight in the grill. There's music, dancing, entertainment, and refreshments, all free of charge. The American Women's Hospitals Reserve Corps is responsible.

THE U.S.O. CLUB, at 1 East 65th Street is sponsored by the Jewish Welfare Board for all non-commissioned men in uniform. The hours are 10:00 a.m. to 11:00 p.m. daily. There's a library, game room and canteen. Entertainment includes weekly dances and Sunday afternoon teas.

THE JANET ROPER CLUB at 3 East 67th Street is operated by the Seaman's Church Institute. It is housed in the beautiful home of one of New York's famous millionaires, the late Thomas Fortune Ryan. There is a lovely garden, two lounges, and an enormous kitchen. Coffee and sandwiches are served at the snack bar. Informal dances are held every Wednesday and Saturday evening. There is never a charge for anything. The club is open from two in the afternoon to eleven at night.

THE COUNCIL CLUB, at 2 East 76th Street, is a canteen run by the National Council of Jewish Women for men of the armed forces and merchant marine of the United Nations. Bed and breakfast is 50c a night. There are recreation facilities including a library and victrola. You can have your mending done here free of charge. The club never closes.

· YORKVILLE ·

EAST 86TH STREET is known as the German Broadway of New York. In the block between 2nd and 3rd Avenues warble Hartz Mountain canary birds, German bands from Hoboken, and deep booming beer bass singers, in spite of the war. However, it would be foolish to say the war has not made a difference to Yorkville, because it has.

The Brau houses, even those run by loyal American-Germans, have suffered from lack of trade. You will see many empty stores and long faces along 86th Street.

It is a wide street, a little down-at-the-heels to be sure, but taking its luck as it comes. The brownstone-front houses which line both sides of the block have seen better days. With false fronts in the form of gaudily painted Bavarian beer-garden entrances camouflaging their prim exteriors, singing waiters clad in bright peasant costumes bring noisy life to their high-ceilinged interiors. The little konditorei shops where neighborhood people go for a cup of coffee and pastry, are also rich in local color.

There are seven brau-houses on East 86th Street between 2nd and 3rd Avenues, from Gloria Palast to Platzl Restaurant.

Yorkville isn't all German. I know at least two excellent Hungarian restaurants in the section. One on East 78th Street just off 2nd Avenue is called Feszek, Hungarian for Nest. You can spot it easily because it is in the Hungarian Theater Building.

The paprika chicken is delicious. The veal chops (when they can get them) are deliciously browned. A full course dinner runs from 80c to $1.50.

At 317 East 79th Street, just a block further north is the Dubrecen, another typical Hungarian restaurant. Mr. Teres presides over the dining room. A spicy aroma floats out from the kitchen where Mrs. Teres presides. Her specialty is goulash chicken. The prices are about like those at the Feszek.

YORKVILLE A.W.V.S., located in the Hotel Carlyle at 981 Madison Avenue, and embracing the entire Yorkville section in its territory, is one of the oldest A.W.V.S. divisions in Greater New York, known as the Tenth from the corresponding Fire Department area. All A.W.V.S. divisions in the city, by the way, are within the boundaries of the Fire Department Battalions. The A.W.V.S. 10th Division, through its Volunteer

Workshop at 33 East 70th Street, pioneered the famous and ever-popular A.W.V.S. Mending and Repair Service for men and women in the armed forces of all the United Nations, a service now also carried on at the A.W.V.S. 11th Division Service Men's Recreation Center at 77th Street and Broadway. Stop in at the 10th Division Workshop at 70th Street and Madison Avenue and perhaps you'll run into a group of soldiers and sailors incongruously attired in A.W.V.S. smocks, contentedly playing a game of cards behind a screen, while women of the division sew buttons on their shirts, shorten their trousers, or press their coats.

· COLUMBIA ·

THE SECTION OF NEW YORK that includes Columbia and the Heights, like other districts in Manhattan, is strong for neighborhood life.

The part of town that has for its boundary-lines 110th Street,

Morningside Drive, 125th Street and Riverside Drive was once given over to pleasant stretches of farmland, the Bloomingdale Asylum and a School for Young Ladies.

Only one building remains of the original asylum unit. It is a quaint brick house, which stands on the Columbia Campus near the chapel and bears the name of East Hall.

A house similar to it once stood at 116th Street and Broadway. Here MacDowell, the famous composer, held his classes for many years, and near here, a tablet tells us, was fought the Battle of Harlem Heights.

Along with the two old buildings the university inherited a gardener from the asylum, who created a great deal of excitement among the students and faculty by referring to them as "the inmates."

Columbia University has grown so large that it is a city in itself. Even in war-time the registry is high. For the semester ending June, 1943, there were 3,698 men and 5,557 women students.

· HARLEM ·

HARLEM is a teeming hotbed of all nations. Italians, negroes, Swedes, Portuguese, Spaniards, Irish and Russians crowd in the narrow streets and cubicled apartment-houses.

The out-of-town visitor thinks of Harlem as a series of negro revues staged from midnight to dawn. This is an aspect, but only one, of the many-sided locality.

I asked Mrs. Gertrude Bolden, negro social worker at the Juvenile Welfare Council to name the places she thought visitors to Harlem might like to see.

"Judging from the out-of-town service men and women to whom I've talked this is about what they like," she said, handing me the following list:

U.S.O. Center at 2348 Seventh Avenue between 137th and 138th Streets. The Saturday night dances are very popular.

The Harlem Y.W.C.A., 179 West 137th Street.

The Harlem Y.M.C.A., 180 West 135th Street. (I recommend the sweet potato pie here.)

The Paul Laurence Dunbar, largest all-negro apartment house in the world, at 2594 Seventh Avenue. Built by the Rockefellers.

Harlem River Houses, 207 West 151st Street. This is a New York City Housing Authority project. There are all too few of this type in Harlem. Just by way of contrast take a look at West 143rd Street between Seventh and Eighth Avenues. Four thousand people are packed into this one block. Mrs. Bolden and I walked through it the week after the last Harlem riot.

ENTERTAINMENT

Small's Paradise, 2294 Seventh Avenue, corner 135th Street (three shows a night. Colored revue).

Murrain's, 2241 Seventh Avenue. A small and intimate supper club. Show people like Bill Robinson go here.

The Old Colony Restaurant, 354 Lenox Avenue at 139th Street, famous for its mint juleps.

Dick Wheaton's, 2339 Seventh Avenue at 137th Street. Good drinks.

The Elks Rendezvous, 464 Lenox Avenue, a tourist night-club spot. Colored and white theatrical people like this place.

The Apollo Theater, 253 West 125th Street.

No visit to Harlem would be complete without a barbecue. The most popular is Eddie Green's Bar-B-Q, 543 Lenox Avenue at 133rd Street. There is also a very good rotisserie at 136th Street and Eighth Avenue where chickens are roasted on the spit.

El Mundial at 222 West 116th Street is a favorite restaurant.

Also the Hotel Theresa at Seventh Avenue and 125th Street for food and drinks.

SPORTS

Harlem's favorite bowling alley is at 116th Street and Lenox Avenue.

The most popular tennis court is at the Cosmopolitan Club, 149th Street and Convent Avenue. Service men are admitted free.

The Colonial, at 145th Street and Edgecomb Avenue, is their best swimming pool.

CHURCHES

PROTESTANT

The Abyssinian Baptist Church, 132 West 138th Street, the largest negro congregation in the world. It numbers between nine and twelve thousand members.

St. Mark's Methodist Church, 49 Edgecomb Avenue.

CATHOLIC

St. Mark's, 65 West 138th Street.

St. Aloysius, 219 West 132nd Street.

JEWISH

Negro Synagogue, 129 West 131st Street.

INTER-DENOMINATIONAL

Father Divine's Palace Mission, 280 West 155th Street.

SETTLEMENT HOUSE

Friendship House, 34 West 135th Street. This is a very inter-esting neighborhood center run by a Russian Baroness.

NEAL'S. The substantial oyster and chop-house of **Harlem** is Neal's at 65 East 125th Street. The restaurant is large and rambling, the atmosphere and food satisfying and the attitude of the waiters reassuring. They are competent and well-fed looking. Dinner for two runs about $3.00.

Harlem is a strange mixture of all nationalities. Broadly speaking, every country in the world is represented in that section of New York which extends from 110th Street north to 150th Street, and that is bounded by Morningside Drive on the west and the East River on the East side.

Among the most law-abiding, deep-thinking groups of people in Harlem are the Finns. They settled some thirty years ago in the blocks around 125th to 127th Streets. They are educated, filled with a deep love of their mother country, and circumspect in their living.

A tiny little square of which few know even in Harlem is Sylvan Place just across from the Harlem Court on East 121st Street. A delicate bit of iron-work forms the high-arched fence that guards it.

The court, like Patchin Place in Greenwich Village, is made up of old-fashioned houses, but in this instance they shelter families who have never moved away from their original homes.

HARLEM A.W.V.S. Well worth a visit is the headquarters of the A.W.V.S. 12th Division at 55 West 125th Street, one of the two branches of the organization in this section of the city.

Further up town at 306 West 136th Street on the ground floor of one of the houses owned by the Urban League are the offices of the A.W.V.S. 16th Division, which also maintains a Volunteer Workshop at 172 West 135th Street where women knit and sew. This division has a fine group of Juniors who once a month entertain the service men at the U.S.O. Club on 7th Avenue between 137th and 138th Streets.

· *WASHINGTON HEIGHTS* ·

THE NORTHWEST SECTION of Manhattan Island takes in the Washington Heights and the Inwood Park section which were once suburbs of New York City. The locality was dotted with the summer homes of rich New Yorkers. Today, the same territory is a solid mass of great apartment buildings.

Fortunately a couple of parks have been salvaged. Inwood Park at the tip end of Manhattan Island is a delightful place to walk. It is still possible to fish for bass from its banks and to explore the Indian caves which honeycomb that portion of the island. This locality was once the camping ground of "Manhattan" Island Indians.

The quickest way to reach Inwood Park is by the Washington Heights division of the 8th Avenue subway to Inwood station. Take the Van Cortlandt Park branch of the West Side subway to 215th Street and Isham Park. The Ishams were an old New York family. The park took its name from the Isham mansion which is used as a local historical museum.

Washington Heights, just to the south of Inwood and Isham Park, has become a vast empire of refugees.

*　*　*.

WASHINGTON HEIGHTS A.W.V.S. Washington Heights is a family neighborhood, famous for its babies. It is quite appropriate, therefore, that the first A.W.V.S. units in the city to use discarded baby carriages for the collection of salvage should have been the five units of the A.W.V.S. 13th Division, known as the Washington Heights, Dyckman, Marble Hill, Inwood and St. Nicholas units.

The headquarters of the A.W.V.S. 13th Division are in a store at 4135 Broadway near 175th Street, and close by, at 4107 Broadway, is the division's very fine Consumer Information Center.

BRONX ZOO & BOTANICAL GARDENS

DON'T go to the Bronx Zoo or Botanical Gardens unless you can spend the day. There are so many animals and birds and flowers to see and so many pleasant paths to follow that no one should attempt it in less time. You can take your own lunch and eat it under the trees or you can get sandwiches and soft drinks at anyone of half a dozen garden lunch counters and beer gardens.

There are several ways of reaching the Bronx Zoo and Botanical Gardens. The quickest is the West Side subway to 180th Street. (Be sure you're on a Bronx train). If you want to dawdle there is the 3rd Avenue El which runs above ground all the way.

The Bronx Zoo puts on a good show for adults and children. The management has a clever manner of dramatizing the exhibits. This week it may be Africa, with all the animals native to Africa grouped around a typical African water-hole. Next week the same territory may be transformed into an Australian country-side with kangaroos leaping about.

Also on dress parade is the children's Zoo, one of the most fascinating exhibits there.

The Botanical Gardens are just as diverting. This year the feature is a model farm.

The
READER'S DIGEST

Articles of Lasting Interest

CHAPTER IV

Our Markets

NEW YORK'S PUBLIC MARKETS are now the largest in the world. Since the war they have become all the more fascinating. Those who explore them will find entertainment, adventure, bargains and close-ups of present day conditions. They will discover strange and exotic foods, be given odd recipes and accumulate a whole new set of picturesque acquaintances with queer romances, amusements and ways. Market people are a friendly lot who respond quickly to interest in themselves and their wares.

Of all the city's 28 markets, the Essex, on the Lower East Side, the Park Avenue, which borders Harlem, and the First Avenue, in the heart of the Italian-Jewish-Roumanian quarter just south of East 14th Street offer the best bargain and character hunting ground.

THE ESSEX MARKET

The Essex is the oldest of the three. Its people are the most discontented and at the same time, the most engaging. Childlike, they tell everybody their troubles. Since 1887 they have been the open-air merchants of the Ghetto. They were the pushcart peddlers of Orchard Street. In November, 1939, the Department of Markets moved them indoors. It wanted to protect shopkeepers who paid store rents. It also wanted to improve the sanitary conditions under which the food was being sold.

Essex Market is still the best place to look for antique jewelry, brasses, musical instruments, lengths of cloth, silverware and unusual gifts. It is also a shopping center for vegetables and groceries. But here, at least to me, that is secondary. Stocks fluctuate. One day you may find everything. Next day, nothing. This element of chance brings a thrill.

Fish for the Fulton Fish Market

The market opens at 7:00 a.m., closes at 7:00 p.m. Twelve noon, the market scene is at its height. Roof-tops echo with the sound of many voices.

The easiest way to reach it is by 3rd Avenue El to Grand Street. When you leave the station walk seven short blocks east and two blocks north. On the northeast corner is the main market building. On the southeast corner is the fish section.

PARK AVENUE MARKET

Conditions, good or bad, don't trouble the venders of the Park Avenue Market. They belong to a different race. Of the 500 who lease stalls, sixty per cent are from Latin America, Puerto Rico and the West Indies. The rest are negroes, chiefly from the Southern states.

The Park Avenue Market is like a Fair. In the streets surrounding it are the following: soda pop and sweet potato men with their carts, fellows with scales who refund your money if they fail to guess your weight, gaudily dressed Gypsy fortune tellers, little darky boys selling market bags, peddlers with bright bits of cheap jewelry, salesmen of penny songs (sometimes they sing them for you), old Italian organ grinders with trained monkeys —and, in the side streets, blatant-fronted perfume shops where voodoo powder and love charms are sold.

FIRST AVENUE MARKET

The First Avenue Market is famous for land snails.

In a remote part of the Bronx, on Arthur Avenue and 183rd Street, just beyond the grim Home for Incurables, lies one of New York's gayest street markets. It is Sicilian. I went there first when the market people were celebrating the feast-day of their patron, St. Anthony.

Pushcarts faced both sidewalks. Usually they flank one. The right side today, the left tomorrow. This is done to bring an equal amount of business to shops on both sides of the streets. Trade lies with the pushcarts.

Women carry huge shopping bags bulging like horns of plenty. Men balance baskets on their heads. Tomatoes, cheese and fish, are the three great commodities of the Italian markets. Snails, squid and a curious pink Conch shell-fish fill the brown wicker baskets in front of fish markets.

Ordinarily, Saturday afternoon is the best time to see Arthur Avenue. But on St. Anthony's feast day, the crowds were so great that it was almost impossible to move. When they carried the Saint through the streets to the chapel of Our Lady of St. Carmel, the mobs billowed back into the stores, dragging baby carriages and shopping baskets out of the way.

HARLEM'S PUSHCART MARKET

It was a bright, sunshiny morning when I went to Harlem's pushcart market.

I found it straggling all the way down one side of 8th Avenue from 143rd to 145th Streets. Everybody was basking in the sun. Perhaps because the people were sleepy, I thought the market quieter than most I'd been to. But it was very nice and the peddlers were friendly. Sweet potatoes, watermelons, okra, rice, gumbo, pork; all the things you find in the South were here, either in the pushcarts or in the stores fronting them. Occasionally, some wandering vender called out, "'Taters, yams, com'n get 'em."

MARKET OF ALL NATIONS

The row of pushcarts extending along the north side of 121st Street between 2nd and 3rd Avenues, is known as The Market of All Nations. It is lots of fun, as well as an excellent shopping center and for an added bit of adventure there is a fascinating junk shop in an arcade at the far end that sells second-hand books, engravings, and even old pianola records. As in all second-hand stores, you may find a treasure here one day and nothing the next.

On 114th Street from 1st to 2nd Avenues you will see a duplicate of this market, more on the Spanish side, perhaps, because of its proximity to the Puerto Rican and Central American districts, but with about the same wares. This market, incidentally, serves one of the most congested and poorest sections of New York.

On 98th Street between 3rd and 1st Avenues is a phantom market as elusive as quick-silver. One moment there are a hundred or more furtive-eyed men bending over little heaps of old clothing, bottles, rusty iron and mangy furs stacked along sidewalks and in vacant lots. If you so much as glance in their direction, clothing, furs, everything, is whisked out of sight and the men stroll casually up the block or lean nonchalantly against tenement walls talking indifferently to one another.

Twenty blocks south of this strange junk market is Yorkville's pushcart row. It wanders along 2nd Avenue from 79th to 72nd Streets along the east side of the avenue, a quaint, picturesque group of tidy carts stocked with everything from fresh vegetables to dressmakers' supplies and sweetmeat stalls. This is a paradise for itinerant musicians and venders as well as the more permanent pushcart peddlers. An old-time band was playing near the start of the market. Further down I stopped an old man carrying a little black box marked Fortune Teller in big, white letters.

On Amsterdam, between 65th and 63rd Streets, I found the city's cheapest produce pushcart market. The quality was high and the values remarkable. The peddlers were chiefly Neapolitans and the customers negroes.

OTHER PUSHCART MARKETS

For color, I recommend Avenue C's pushcart market. This has a great deal of the character of the old Orchard Street market before it was moved indoors. Vegetables are the least part. Stretching its noisy length from 9th to 5th Streets it is the most interesting outdoor market in New York and the least exploited. Peddlers and customers are practically all neighborhood people. It has the flavor of an Oriental bazaar; street cries, strange wares, odd characters and remarkable bargains. It also has the customs of the East.

Like Essex Market, brass candlesticks and amber beads are sold here. The best values are at Uncle Clang's, the pawnbroker, whose shop faces the carts at 156 Avenue C.

Another fascinating market with a foreign quality rambles along Mott Street from Hester to Broome Streets. Here the Sicilians meet the Chinese. I found strange new vegetables in these carts. One called cande, was a cross between zuccini and celery. A friendly Italian housewife told me she cooked it in olive oil. There were also whole pushcarts full of nuts. Stopping to price a cheese resting in a beautiful hand-woven basket, I heard someone singing. The song which floated out over the street was punctuated by a tapping.

"Who is that?" I asked my peddler.

"The blind man," he said.

Quite as picturesque in its way, though not so varied as to stock, are the two Italian pushcart markets of Greenwich Village. One runs along Bleecker from Downing to Christopher Streets. The other cuts north on Thompson Street in the heart of the wholesale artificial flower district. Here, you find entertainment in the customers, as well as the peddlers. Artists from the Village wander through at odd times, hunting for bargains, especially at the Bleecker Street market. On Thompson Street you are apt to meet students from New York University who live in the neighborhood.

CHAPTER V

Our Churches

There are 290 churches in New York — too many to name more than the principal ones of each denomination.

BAPTIST
> RIVERSIDE, 122nd Street and Riverside Drive.

CHRISTIAN SCIENCE
> FIRST CHURCH OF CHRIST, SCIENTIST, Central Park West and 96th Street.

CONGREGATIONAL
> TABERNACLE, Broadway and 56th Street.

JEWISH
> TEMPLE EMANU-EL, 5th Avenue and 65th Street.

LUTHERAN
> ST. PETER's Lexington Avenue and 54th Street.

METHODIST EPISCOPAL
> CHRIST CHURCH, 60th Street and Park Avenue.

PRESBYTERIAN
> FIFTH AVENUE PRESBYTERIAN CHURCH, 5th Avenue and 55th Street.

QUAKER
> FRIENDS' MEETING HOUSE, 144 East 20th Street.

PROTESTANT EPISCOPAL
> CATHEDRAL OF ST. JOHN THE DIVINE, West 111th Street between Amsterdam and Morningside Avenues.

REFORMED CHURCH
> MARBLE COLLEGIATE, 5th Avenue at 29th Street.

ROMAN CATHOLIC
> ST. PATRICK's CATHEDRAL, 5th Avenue at East 50th Street.

RUSSIAN ORTHODOX
> CHURCH OF CHRIST THE SAVIOR, 51 East 121st Street.

HISTORICAL
> ST. PAUL's CHAPEL, Broadway and Fulton Street.
> TRINITY CHURCH, Broadway and Wall Street.

CHAPTER VI

Our Museums

AMERICAN MUSEUM OF NATURAL HISTORY, Central Park West at 77th Street. Open Mondays through Saturdays from 10 a.m. to 5 p.m. Sundays 1-5 p.m. *Admission free.*

THE CLOISTERS (a branch of the Metropolitan Museum of Art devoted to medieval art) Fort Tryon Park. Open Mondays through Saturdays from 10 a.m. to 5 p.m. Sundays 1 to 6 p.m. *Admission free* except on Mondays and Fridays when there is a charge of 25c.

FRICK COLLECTION, 1 East 70th Street. Museum of paintings, sculpture, enamels, porcelains and period furniture. Open Mondays through Saturdays from 10 a.m. to 5 p.m. Sundays and holidays 1 to 5 p.m. *Admission free.*

GUGGENHEIM GALLERY, Museum of Non-Objective Painting, 24 East 54th Street. Open Tuesdays through Saturdays from 10 a.m. to 6 p.m. Sundays from 12 noon to 6 p.m. Closed Mondays. *Admission free.*

HAYDEN PLANETARIUM, 81st Street near Central Park West. *Admission 30c in the afternoon and 40c in the evening.* Service men and service women admitted free at all times.

METROPOLITAN MUSEUM OF ART, 5th Avenue at 82nd Street. Open Mondays through Saturdays from 10 a.m. to 5 p.m. Sundays 1 to 6 p.m. *Admission free.*

MORGAN LIBRARY, 33 East 36th Street. Open Mondays through Saturdays from 10 a.m. to 5 p.m. Closed Sundays and month of August. *Admission free.*

MUSEUM OF THE AMERICAN INDIAN, HEYE FOUNDATION, 155th Street and Broadway. Open Mondays through Saturdays from 2 to 5 p.m. Closed Sundays, holidays and months of July and August. *Admission free.*

MUSEUM OF THE CITY OF NEW YORK, 5th Avenue at 103rd Street. Open daily except Tuesdays, 10 a.m. to 5 p.m. Sundays 1 to 5 p.m. *Admission free.*

MUSEUM OF MODERN ART, 11 West 53rd Street. Open weekdays 10 a.m. to 6 p.m. except Wednesdays when it is open from 10 a.m. to 10 p.m. Sundays from 12 to 6 p.m. *Admission 25c.*

NEW YORK HISTORICAL SOCIETY GALLERY AND MUSEUM, Central Park West between 76th and 77th Streets. Museum open Tuesdays through Saturdays from 10 a.m. to 5 p.m. Sundays 1 to 5 p.m. Closed Mondays.

OLD MERCHANT'S HOUSE, 29 East 4th Street between Lafayette Street and Bowery. Open Mondays through Saturdays from 11 a.m. to 5 p.m. Sundays and holidays from 1 to 5 p.m. *Admission 50c.*

POE COTTAGE, Poe Park, Kingsbridge Road and Grand Concourse, Bronx. Open daily from 10 a.m. to 1 p.m. and 2 p.m. to 5 p.m. except Sundays 1 p.m. to 5 p.m. Closed Mondays. *Admission free.*

ROGER MORRIS HOUSE (Jumel Mansion), Edgecombe Avenue and West 160th Street. Open daily except Mondays, 11 a.m. to 5 p.m. *Admission free.*

ROOSEVELT HOUSE, 28 East 20th Street (birthplace of Theodore Roosevelt). Open Tuesdays through Saturdays 10 a.m. to 5 p.m. Sundays and holidays, 1 to 5 p.m. *Admission free* except on Wednesdays and Fridays when there is a charge of 25c.

CHAPTER VII

Our Public Buildings

Here are the locations of the public buildings you will want to see. There are many others but not the space to name them:

STATUE OF LIBERTY, Bedloe's Island.
> Boats leave the Battery every hour on the hour each day until six o'clock. Round trip fare 35c. There is no charge to climb up into the arm of the Statue, but if you want to ride in the elevator, it costs 5c.

CUSTOMS HOUSE, Bowling Green.
> Open 9 a.m. to 5 p.m.

SUB-TREASURY BUILDING, Broad and Wall Streets.
> The large statue of George Washington at entrance commemorates the fact that on this spot he took the oath of office as President of the United States.

CITY HALL, Manhattan.
> One of the loveliest structures in New York. The interior is Colonial.

FEDERAL BUILDING, 90 Church Street.
> U. S. Army and Navy Information.

NEW YORK PUBLIC LIBRARY, 5th Avenue and 42nd Street.
> Open daily 9 a.m. to 10 p.m.; Sundays from 1 to 10 p.m.

BRONX PARK.
> The grounds are open at all times. Zoo opens daily at 10 a.m. Admission Tuesdays, Wednesdays and Thursdays, 11c for adults, 5c for children. Other days free. Botanical Garden. Museum building is open daily from 10 a.m. to 4:30 p.m. The Conservatories are open daily from 10 a.m. to 4 p.m. The grounds and buildings are free to the public every day.

COLLEGES AND UNIVERSITIES

In another part of the book both Columbia and New York Universities have been mentioned. Here are others which you may want to visit:

BARNARD COLLEGE, Broadway and 119th Street.

THE COLLEGE OF THE CITY OF NEW YORK, Convent Avenue and 139th Street.

FORDHAM UNIVERSITY, Fordham Road, Bronx.

HUNTER COLLEGE, 696 Park Avenue.

TEACHERS COLLEGE, 525 West 120th Street.

HOSPITALS

New York has eighty-six hospitals. Of these the best known are:

BELLEVUE, (the city's biggest hospital), at the foot of East 26th Street.

COLUMBIA PRESBYTERIAN MEDICAL CENTER, (the largest hospital unit in the world), Broadway and 168th Street.

NEW YORK HOSPITAL, (adjoining Cornell Medical Center), 525 East 68th Street.

ROOSEVELT HOSPITAL, 59th Street and 9th Avenue.

The leading sectarian hospitals are:

MOUNT SINAI, (Jewish), 5th Avenue and 100th Street.

ST. LUKE'S, (Episcopalian), Amsterdam Avenue and 115th Street.

ST. VINCENT'S, (Catholic), 7th Avenue and 11th Street.

*   *   *

THE STORY OF NEW YORK is never fully told. That is part of the city's charm. You will never know it completely. There is always more to see. And what you have seen changes. Even by the time this book is published some of the little shops and quaint characters I have mentioned may be gone. But you will find others, equally interesting, to take their place. When you do, write me so that we may put them in the next edition for others to enjoy.